The GREAT & *the* GOOD

JOHN GILES
The GREAT
& *the* GOOD

**THE LEGENDARY PLAYERS, MANAGERS
& TEAMS OF FIFTY FOOTBALL YEARS**

with

Declan Lynch

*Best Wishes
John Giles*

HACHETTE
BOOKS
IRELAND

First published in 2012 by Hachette Books Ireland
First published in paperback in 2013 by Hachette Books Ireland.
A division of Hachette UK Ltd.

A CIP catalogue record for this title is available from the British Library.

ISBN 978 1 44474 363 0

Inside design and typeset by Bookends Publishing Services
Cover design by AmpVisual.com
Cover author photo by Emily Quinn

Printed and bound in Great Britain by
CPI Group (UK) Ltd, Croydon, CR0 4YY

Hachette Books Ireland policy is to use papers that are natural, renewable and recyclable products and made from wood grown in sustainable forests. The logging and manufacturing processes are expected to conform to the environmental regulations of the country of origin.

Hachette Books Ireland
8 Castlecourt Centre
Castleknock
Dublin 15, Ireland

A division of Hachette UK Ltd
338 Euston Road
London NW1 3BH
www.hachette.ie

Contents

Foreword

Asked late in his career what his greatest mistake had been, Sir Matt Busby didn't pause for a second before admitting that it was allowing John Giles to leave Old Trafford. The great man was canny. He didn't give hostages to fortune. Or easily own up to mistakes or misgivings.

On the subject of Giles, Busby's regret was profound. For he understood that when he sold Giles to Leeds United, he lost not just a great footballer but a football man of immense character who possessed a rare understanding of the game.

Many great players work off intuition. They are naturals with the gifts of power, pace, guile and vision. They impose themselves on games by sheer brilliance. Think George Best, Maradona or Lionel Messi, Bobby Charlton or Giles' Leeds team-mate, Billy Bremner.

Others bring different, more cerebral qualities to battle. Franz Beckenbauer, Johan Cruyff, Spain's two maestros Xavi and

Iniesta, Bobby Moore and the majestic Pelé graced football with extraordinary intelligence. Giles belongs in this category.

At its most inspiring, football is about applied intelligence, about knowing what you've got, what the opposition has and understanding how to win even if the others are technically better than you. Even on a bad day.

The game as played by Giles could occasionally be about a moment of divine inspiration, the killer pass or the dazzling strike on goal. But more often football as he understood it was a sustained mental battle, probing, posing questions of your opponent, testing his powers of concentration and ultimately breaking the will of lesser men.

We are blessed today to bear witness in the form of Spain and Barcelona to a version of football that really is the beautiful game.

Although there are wonderful bursts of explosive brilliance – think Messi again – what is most extraordinary and impossible for opponents to withstand is the sophistry of glorious passing and intelligent movement, the apparently simple rendered beautiful.

This is the football Giles has always envisaged as long as I have known him. It's the football he played and evangelised when later coaching. Most of all it's the football we grew up dreaming about. We were materially poor but rich in our imagination, knowing what was possible with nothing more than a ball and native wit.

More than anyone I've ever known, John Giles understands the game of football. He doesn't just see what's happening in a game, he sees what didn't happen but could have if a different pass was played, a different run was made, another angle tested, play switched at a critical moment.

His greatness as a player was informed by his knowledge of all the possibilities of any given moment in any contest. For this gift, he was uniquely respected within the game in the glorious era he graced with so many other great players.

As a television analyst, John is peerless. He sees the game in 3D; the rest of us are watching the ball. What really matters in a football match usually is happening off the ball. To see the full picture you need 20/20 vision and then some. Which is precisely what John possesses.

John is undemonstrative by nature. But his passion for the game is real and deeply felt. He has taken football analysis to a new level and in the process enriched the experience of watching games not just for RTÉ's audience but for those of us fortunate to work with him.

For all other passions – cinema, theatre, literature, rock 'n' roll, fine wine and good food – rigorous criticism enhances our experience, makes us reflect upon and question our beliefs. The same rigour should be applied to soccer. Which is what John sets out to do in this fascinating book. There is nobody better equipped to make that most important distinction between the good and the great.

Eamon Dunphy
July 2012

Introduction

It was 1984, Eamon Dunphy was on the RTÉ panel for the European Championship being played in France. Michel Platini, the captain of the host nation, was playing brilliantly and France were on course to win the tournament, which they duly did. Most commentators remember the tournament as a story in which an outstanding team, led by the inspiring Platini, finally claimed what was rightfully theirs, after various misfortunes and injustices had done them down – most notably in the semi-final of the 1982 World Cup when the Frenchman Patrick Battiston, having been put through on goal by Platini, was met by the German goalkeeper Harald Schumacher who raced out of his box and almost killed Battiston in the ensuing collision as the Frenchman attempted to lob the ball into the net. France had gone 3–1 up in extra-time, but the Germans came back, as they tend to do, and when the game ended in a 3–3 draw they won the penalty shootout, again as they tend to do. Outside of Germany itself, the whole world had wanted France to win that thrilling game, and to win the final with this hugely talented team featuring Marius Trésor, Alain Giresse, Dominique Rocheteau, Jean Tigana and Platini himself.

Two years later, it looked as if they were about to claim their destiny, in their own country, finally confirming their greatness and particularly the greatness of their leader, Michel Platini.

This, at least, was the accepted way of looking at it, the version in which the French finally got their reward, leading to a happy ending for all concerned. But on RTÉ, Eamon Dunphy was looking at it differently. And he was starting to get into a bit of trouble as a result.

Platini, he maintained, was not a great player. He was a good player … not a great player.

And as luck would have it, the more that Eamon insisted that Platini was not a great player, the more Platini seemed determined to prove that he was indeed a great player, doing all the things that great players are inclined to do, such as scoring nine goals in five games in the tournament, including the opening goal in the final against Spain, and generally doing all sorts of brilliant things which only made Eamon's position more difficult to sustain with each passing day.

But sustain it he did, until the bitter end and beyond. It was one of the first major controversies of his career in journalism, and while we didn't know it at the time, it would give rise to a catchphrase which is still widely used in Ireland to this day – 'a good player, not a great player' is the basis of many jokes and many headlines, not just about football but in relation to matters well beyond the sport. These days, it never fails to get a laugh when some version of it is used by a presenter or a politician, but like a lot of these things there was a certain truth at the heart of it.

I had not joined the RTÉ panel at the time – I eventually joined it for the 1986 World Cup – but I broadly agreed with Eamon's verdict on Platini. I had played against Platini, and I had no doubt that he was a brilliant player. When the Republic of Ireland lost to France in a World Cup qualifier in Paris, he had an outstanding game, but in the return leg, on a blustery day at Lansdowne Road, we beat them. And Platini went missing. The game was a bit physical, the conditions were tricky and I don't think he responded.

Greatness is a combination of many things. It is about talent and brilliance and the ability to make the crowd gasp in amazement, but it is not about these things alone. It is also about being able to do it on a blustery day on a bumpy pitch, when nobody really feels like doing it. I felt that Platini failed that test at Lansdowne. When judged by the very highest standards, this revealed a weakness that you don't see in the truly great players. So when Eamon applied the most rigorous standards to Platini, even in the context of a tournament in which he was becoming the star man, I felt he was doing the right thing. And when I joined the RTÉ panel, we both tried to apply these standards in the years that followed and up to the present day.

But why would we bother with these distinctions between the great and the good? What does it matter if a player has a wonderful career which makes a lot of people happy but is perhaps not up there with the very best of all time? Are some of the critics right – are we just being grumpy old men?

I don't think so.

First of all, I wouldn't want to take anything away from the brilliance of a player like Michel Platini or, to give a modern example, Ryan Giggs. It is important to state that they have been terrific players over the years, and that the game is better off for their contributions. So I certainly don't want to detract anything from what they have achieved in their careers. At the same time, I don't want to detract from the players who are, in my opinion, the truly great ones. That is the most important thing to me, especially in these times when so many commentators are out there heaping praise on all and sundry, hyping things up at all times, telling us that everything – and everybody – is great.

Because if everybody is great, nobody is great.

I've always felt that we need to get these things right in football, just like they do when they're talking about the greatest writers of all time or the greatest film-makers or whatever. For example, people talk in a different way about Shakespeare than they do about anyone else who has ever written the English language. They feel it would be wrong to put him on the same level as other writers who do not have his genius, who are just very good at what they do.

I believe that football should revere its true greats in much the same way, that we should try to really understand what makes them so special, while not forgetting players such as Platini and Ryan Giggs and Steven Gerrard who are exceptionally gifted lads. And by true greats here I mean the managers as well as the players, and the teams that they created.

Even as a kid, I was terrifically interested in the players that everyone used to talk about – Wilf Mannion, Stanley Matthews, Dixie Dean or Raich Carter. In Ireland, we couldn't actually see most of them, apart from the odd glimpse that we might get in an exhibition game. Obviously there was no TV analysis, so I listened to people talking about them but I was never really satisfied with what I heard.

I couldn't find out why exactly they were so special – in fact, this frustrates me to this day because I still haven't found out.

I knew that Len Shackleton, for example, who played for Newcastle United and Sunderland in the 1940s and 1950s, was called the 'Clown Prince' for his antics, such as back-heeling a penalty kick into the goal or taunting the opposition by putting his foot on the ball and pretending to comb his hair. Later, he was best known for his autobiography in which he had a chapter entitled 'What The Average Director Knows About Football', which consisted of a blank page.

So I knew these things about Len Shackleton, without ever really knowing if he was any good or not. Was he one of these 'entertainers' like Duncan McKenzie or Frank Worthington, or was he better than that? It's still a bit of a mystery, but we know that Shackleton is usually mentioned alongside the likes of Wilf Mannion, as if they were all roughly of the same high standard. I always wanted to know more.

And this vagueness doesn't just apply to football. I have often found it very frustrating that we don't really know enough about the great golfers or tennis players or boxers or whatever. I would love to hear, say, Tom Watson talk in detail about Ben Hogan or John McEnroe analyse the play of Rod Laver, so I would know exactly why they were great rather than just hearing that they were legends of the game. I always had a huge curiosity about these things and my interest is as strong now as it ever was. I was very taken with the view of the renowned golf coach Bob Torrance, who made this distinction between a good golfer and a great golfer. 'A good golfer can play great golf when he's in the right mood. A great golfer can play great golf when he wants to.'

As for those old-timers, such as Wilf Mannion, of whom we know so little, the way they were treated and the poverty they endured at the end of their days still makes me angry. Mannion, in all likelihood, was a truly great player for Middlesbrough. From all that I have heard about him, his reputation was fully deserved, unlike a few of the players I saw when I first came over to England, who were getting credit that they shouldn't really have been getting. Certainly Mannion used to attract massive crowds on his name alone, making fortunes for other people in the process while he was still receiving the maximum wage – and probably being told he was lucky to be getting anything at all, playing football when everyone else had to go down the mines. Maybe if Mannion had been properly appreciated, if his greatness had been analysed and acknowledged in the right way, his story might have had a happier ending. But he was 'only a footballer', which was regarded as a much more trivial thing than a great singer or even a great politician.

So I can only write with certainty about the ones I've seen, trying to unravel the mystery of what made Bobby Charlton the greatest player I have ever played with or against. Or why there must be a special place in the history of the game for Beckenbauer or Kenny Dalglish or Diego Maradona or John Charles or John Robertson, or Xavi, Messi and Iniesta.

By naming just a few of them, I am again struck by something that has always amazed me, and which deepens the mystery – they are all different. And they are different in so many ways. If you were to see Diego Maradona standing beside Franz Beckenbauer, and you didn't know anything about them, you'd never think that they were in the same line of work at all. And as players they were so different. Just as the managers are different – Alex Ferguson and Matt Busby and Brian Clough and Don Revie all had different strengths, and maybe a few weaknesses too which were unique in their own way.

John Robertson, who played under Clough at Nottingham Forest, may be in a category all of his own because to my mind he was a great player who is almost never acknowledged as such. Indeed when I have mentioned him alongside the likes of Cruyff and Pelé, people have assumed that I must have made a mistake, and have corrected me for it – I have to point out that there is no mistake, that I feel that Robertson really deserves to be there, for reasons which I will be happy to explain later.

They are all so different, and yet they all have this one mysterious thing in common, this quality we call greatness. When I was a small boy, I was inspired by stories of these players, like Jackie Carey and Stanley Matthews, players I knew instinctively were special. And when I achieved my dream of becoming a professional footballer, playing with or against the likes of Denis Law and Johnny Haynes, I thought about it more deeply. I realised that apart from their outstanding talent, there were certain fundamental things that they all had – things like honesty of effort, the moral courage to take responsibility at all times, the intelligence and humility not to be publicly remonstrating with colleagues and to play the simple pass when that is the right thing to do.

Playing the simple pass may sound easy, but for some it is too easy. I remember a young lad in the reserves at Shamrock Rovers who was told on numerous ocasions that when the full-back went on the overlap he should just give the ball to him. And yet for a long time he seemed unable to do this, which was baffling to me and to everyone else.

'What is going through your head when you don't give it to him?' I said.

Eventually he blurted out the reason: 'It's too fucking easy.'

'Pelé is the best player in the world,' I explained, 'and it wouldn't be too easy for him.'

For the great players, nothing is too simple, they are not trying to show off. There is so much that goes into it, and we only realise how hard it is to maintain those standards when we see how quickly it can all go wrong. A couple of years ago, for example, it was automatically assumed that Wayne Rooney and Fernando Torres would continue to do what they had always done in the Premier League, playing brilliantly and scoring goals and generally adding lustre to their reputations. And then suddenly it all seemed to go wrong for both of them, in ways that nobody would have foreseen. Rooney's performances for Manchester United and England were getting worse at a time when everyone felt they would be getting better, and there were fears that he might never get back to where he was. A player who seemed destined for a place alongside the football immortals was hugely diminished for the best part of a season, by troubles that are ultimately known only to himself and to those closest to him.

As for Torres, he had other problems – injuries, and the ownership controversies that threatened to destroy Liverpool FC, brought him down to such an extent that he seemed desperate to leave Anfield, where he had so recently been regarded as a god. Then he went to Chelsea for £50 million looking for a fresh start and things, if anything, got worse.

And it is not just footballers who see their careers unravelling in the most unlikely ways. The case of Tiger Woods is probably the most spectacular example of this. Like Rooney or Torres, Tiger seemed like a totally safe bet to continue what he had started, winning his Majors until he equalled Jack Nicklaus' record, before carrying on and winning Majors more or less indefinitely until he reached old age, which is all that could stop him. Of course, as we know, it got a bit more complicated than that.

Which tells us another thing about this quality we call greatness – it is taken for granted. The misfortunes of Rooney and Torres and Woods show that there is so much that goes into it, and so much that can bring it down. It is so fragile. Which means we should appreciate all the more the ones who achieve it, and who manage to hang on to it in spite of all the dangers, all the madness out there.

Perhaps we tend to take any sort of excellence for granted, because in any walk of life things can look so easy when they're done the right way. Franz Beckenbauer looked so relaxed on the pitch, people might have formed the impression that anyone could stroll around like that, making easy passes and generally controlling the game. But having played against Beckenbauer in the European Cup final of 1975, I was struck, not by any laid-back manner of his, but by how devastatingly quick he was. Indeed it was his speed, allied to his great technique and vision, which made the space for him, and which gave him so much time on the ball, creating the illusion that he was just an easy-going fellow playing a simple game.

That was Beckenbauer's way of being a great player but, as we shall see, there are many other ways. And the great players keep coming, even in these cynical times, and they keep inspiring us.

During the early months of 2011, I spent most of my weekends travelling around Ireland helping to organise the Walk of Dreams – a display of unity on the part of the soccer community of Ireland that would raise funds for the development of the game in poorer areas. And from the smallest boy who participated to the oldest man, we all had this love of football and we all had some perfect vision of how the game should be played. I grew up wanting to emulate men like Jackie Carey, the Dubliner who won the 1948 FA Cup with Manchester United and was Footballer of the Year in 1949. The kids on the Walk of Dreams probably feel like that about Lionel Messi – it's the same thing really and, who knows, maybe somewhere on the Walk of Dreams there was another Lionel Messi, or someone who will achieve what Messi has achieved, but in his own way.

I believe there is an old Jewish saying: 'Greatness can come from anywhere.'

1

Matthews or Finney?

My father spent quite a lot of his time in the pubs of Dublin, talking about football with other football men. I know this, because sometimes I would be with him, and I would be listening to their conversations. In fact mostly it boiled down to the same conversation, or the same argument, about who was the best player of the time in the English First Division – Matthews or Finney?

This seems a fairly normal debate for football men to be having, except for one thing – they hardly ever saw Stanley Matthews or Tom Finney, either in real life or on the screen. Not that this prevented them from having very strong opinions on the subject or from expressing those opinions with total conviction.

Relying mainly on newspaper reports and the odd commentary on a crackly wireless, they never questioned their own authority in these matters. They might see a few highlights of the FA Cup final on the Pathé newsreel in the cinema, but otherwise they were able to form their opinions almost entirely without the aid of moving pictures.

Matthews or Finney? Looking back on it now, it seems a bit like picking your favourite colour. But of course these football men were deadly serious about it, so maybe it was more like a matter of religion, with Matthews and Finney each having their followers who worshipped at the shrine without really knowing why.

So my own view of Matthews or Finney is seen mostly through the eyes of a child, based on the evidence of men who had never seen either play. It was a different world.

When you develop as a person, and in my case as a player, your standards change. When I was a kid, I might have seen someone like Rodney Marsh and thought he was a great player, another Matthews or Finney, but you're always evolving as a person, just as the game is evolving.

Back in the time of Matthews and Finney, each player had a position. A right-winger was a right-winger, and nothing else. Today a midfield player can be one of four; back then, the roles were more strictly defined. But the main difference overall between players then and now is probably the level of pressure that they play under. Back then, the pressure wasn't quite as intense as it was for the players – especially the great players – who came in the years that followed, and up until the present day.

It couldn't have been. Admittedly my own career was only beginning when the era of Matthews and Finney was ending, but some of the basic structures of the game meant that it was slightly less pressurised. For a start, there weren't the same financial pressures to win the league. It was the FA Cup that was the huge competition at the time, almost the way the Champions League is today. Off the top of my head, I could name you the cup winners from the 1940s up until the late 1970s, but I'd have to think a lot harder to recall the league winners in that same period.

In fact, wherever you finished in the league, there was no extra financial reward either for club or player. And until Matt Busby and Manchester United defied the authorities by entering the European Cup in 1957, there was no qualification for Europe. It might seem completely bizarre now, but back then the FA was absolutely opposed to clubs entering this new European Cup. The year before Busby went against them, Chelsea had obeyed the wishes of the FA and stayed out of the competition. In fact, the FA thought that it owned the game of football, and England had not even played in the first World Cup in 1930.

I remember going to see Manchester United playng at Maine Road in the European Cup, because for the first couple of years that they played in it, they had no floodlights at Old Trafford. Not even the famous 6–3 defeat of England at Wembley by a brilliant Hungary team in 1953 had fully shaken the FA out of its smug complacency. So while men like Busby were trying to move the game forward, a lot of people were quite happy the way they were. When I was a kid, Huddersfield

Town were a very good team, usually finishing fourth or fifth
in the league, while Burnley with Jimmy McIlroy were also
very good, winning the league in 1960. And one of the reasons
why teams like Huddersfield and Burnley were doing so well
was the maximum wage, which meant that all players were on
roughly the same money – so a player at Burnley was better off
than a player at Arsenal or Tottenham simply because it was
cheaper to live in Burnley than in London.

The pressures were also different at the bottom of the
table. Relegation wasn't the disaster it is today. It didn't cost
the club £50 million. In 2012, Liverpool finished eighth in the
Premier League and it was regarded as a terrible season. If
they had finished eighth in the league in the 1950s, the reaction
would have been, so what? And you didn't have the same level
of attention from the press either, making it a different life
all round. So even if you went down, often you could bounce
back with the same players, because the best ones wouldn't
necessarily be sold. In fact Everton, with excellent players such
as Peter Farrell and Tommy Eglington, were relegated in 1954,
but the club didn't go into oblivion the way that Coventry City
or Sheffield Wednesday have done in recent times – they came
straight back the following season.

Blackpool with Matthews and the captain Harry Johnston
had a terrific team at that time, winning that famous cup final
against Bolton in 1953. But as long as they had a good run in
the cup, even if they didn't win the league, they felt they were
doing well. It was the glory on the day at Wembley that really
mattered.

The supporters had a much different attitude back then

too, which again lessened the pressure on the top players just a bit. When they went to a match, they were highly aware of what the visiting team might have to offer. For example, West Bromwich Albion with Ray Barlow and Ronnie Allen won the cup in 1954. But if Spurs were playing at West Brom, the home fans would be looking forward to seeing the likes of Danny Blanchflower, Bill Nicholson, Eddie Baily, Ronnie Burgess and Alf Ramsey, nearly as much as they'd be looking forward to seeing Barlow and Allen.

In fact Jack Pettitt, a friend of mine and a West Brom supporter who grew up in that era, told me that he recently went to see a match in the play-offs at Wembley and was appalled by the lack of appreciation of the opposition, the way that the supporters from the start were pointing to the other team's fans and chanting abuse at them. They didn't really care about the match at all, it was only about winning. He could recall the days when a member of the opposition would actually be applauded if they did something good.

I can remember those days myself, and even with the much greater pressures which arrived in the 1960s and 1970s, in certain quarters at least there were a slightly more relaxed attitude. Not that it was ever easy-osy. You had the hatchet-men at every club, but players such as Tony Currie, Frank Worthington and Duncan McKenzie were always able to display their skills to an extent, without being expected to win things as well. Tony Currie was a very gifted lad, but his Sheffield United were never going to win anything – then again, they weren't going to be relegated either.

So Currie could express himself in a way that you couldn't

do when you were going for the title, when the last nine or ten games brought this unbelievable pressure down on you. At which point, you'd discover the players who could perform under that pressure and the ones who could not. And those players who could perform would have been around too in the 1940s and 1950s, it's just that the differences in the game back then makes it hard to identify them.

But I have no doubt that Jimmy Scoular was one of them. He was a Scottish international, and a great player for Portsmouth, winning the league twice with them.

The first time I heard about Scoular, I was a small boy listening to my father talking about him with his friend Con Martin, who was a centre-half for Aston Villa at that time. And the two men were describing an incident in which Scoular was verbally abusing Peter Doherty, the outstanding inside-left from Magherafelt in County Derry who played for Manchester City. Scoular had apparently called Doherty 'a Catholic bastard'.

I was shocked by this, though my father and Con Martin seemed to be pretty relaxed about it, and of course little did I know that I would exchange such colourful greetings and maybe a lot worse with various opponents during my own career. Doherty, by the way, was said by some to be the best player of his time – but again, they didn't really say why.

Scoular went from Portsmouth to Newcastle, and captained them to one of their three-in-a-row cup wins in the early 1950s. He was the sort of player who'd drive a team, a right-half, and in fact I played against him for Manchester United at the start of my career and towards the end of his. He had this reputation as a digger, as big a reputation in that department as, say, Peter Storey of Arsenal would have later on. But very early in that game I can clearly remember Scoular picking up the ball in the right-half position and, to my amazement, pinging it forty yards straight to the left-winger's feet. And there was I, because of the stories I had heard, thinking that he couldn't play.

Jimmy Scoular could play all right. And it was one of the biggest thrills of that season of 1959 when I made it into the United first team, that I played against some of these guys that I'd only read or heard about. Perhaps because, growing up in Dublin, I saw so few of them as a kid – I never saw Jackie Milburn, Bobby Mitchell or Joe Harvey – I was always hugely interested in them.

I asked Tommy Eglington about Alf Ramsey, who had been a top-class player. 'Eggo' was a left-winger, very quick, up against the right-back Ramsey. And because the positions were so clearly defined, if you were a winger, you'd be judged on how you played against the full-back on the day. And Tommy Eglington told me that he loved playing against Ramsey, because Ramsey was a good footballer but he wasn't quick. So with his speed, Tommy felt that he could always win that particular contest.

As a kid, I had actually seen Harry Johnston, the captain of Blackpool when they won the Matthews final in 1953, playing in an exhibition match at Dalymount Park. And I thought he was terrific, especially because he was a left-footed player who played right-half. I also saw Roy Bentley playing in a couple of exhibition matches at Dalymount. Bentley played with

Chelsea when they won the league in 1955. He was aggressive, a great header of the ball, a centre-forward, a target man. But he couldn't half play. Also through the eyes of a child, I saw that famous West Bromwich Albion pair Ray Barlow and Ronnie Allen playing for the English league against the Irish league, and I loved watching them play, even if I wasn't properly aware of what I was seeing. I just thought they were brilliant. I would see them much later playing against Manchester United in the sixth round of the FA Cup just after the Munich disaster, when the first match ended in a 2–2 draw and United won the replay 1–0. They are West Brom legends to this day.

The Barlow I remember was a tall man, a left-half with brilliant control and top-notch technique. He was really stylish around the ball, with excellent distribution. And so was Ronnie Allen. He was one of the deep-lying centre-forwards of the time, with a great shot in his left foot and good control. He got a few more caps than Barlow, who only played once for his country, but again we must remember that we're dealing with different times here, in which neither of these players were automatic choices for England. A so-called Selection Committee picked the team, and under this system Billy Wright and Jimmy Dickinson were the regular wing-halves. There were also fewer international matches at the time, and the English game had very few foreign players in it, which meant there was a different dynamic at international level.

Billy Wright was a wing-half with Wolves who, along with Tottenham, were the outstanding team of my childhood. But

I never actually saw Wright play at wing-half. Apparently he had been an all-action player, though I didn't really know the sort of player he was until the first time I saw him play in 1957. United had got to the cup final, and the staff were taken down to London, where, on the Friday, we saw a match at Highbury between Young England and Old England – Wright was the captain of Old England. I went to the match with some of the young United players and saw Wright playing at centre-half. It may have been a friendly, but I thought he was absolutely brilliant. He was only five foot eight inches but he won everything in the air. In fact, he won everything in the game. I met him after he had retired and he was a gentleman.

That night I also saw Eddie Baily of Spurs playing for the first time, another of my heroes that I had heard about over the years. A traditional inside-left, I thought he was brilliant too.

When I first came over to Manchester, I saw the Manchester City team which reached the cup final in 1955 and won it in 1956. They were a terrific side, with an inside-forward called Bobby Johnstone who came from Hibernian in Scotland and eventually went back to Hibs. There was Ken Barnes, an outstanding wing-half whose son Peter was a winger who also played for City. And then there was a certain Don Revie, Footballer of the Year in 1955, who was thought to be bringing something new to the game in the deep-lying centre-forward role, which was known to some as the 'Revie Plan'. Much later, Don told me about another City player that I didn't see, the Welsh international right-half Roy Paul. Don raved about him.

City had a legendary goalkeeper too in Bert Trautmann. I played against him, and I can confirm that there was more to Trautmann than the one thing he is most famous for – his heroism in playing a large part of the 1956 FA Cup final with a broken neck. In fact, that story was so remarkable that Trautmann was in danger of becoming something of a Len Shackleton figure, widely known as a bit of a character but at the end of it all still begging the question: was he any good?

I found it hugely frustrating that I hadn't been able to get a proper rundown on the true abilities of players such as Trautmann, a sense of what they were really like. In fact, Trautmann was a great goalkeeper. He was brave, of course, but he was also very athletic, and he distributed the ball brilliantly. He would throw it from the shoulder, picking out the inside-forward something in the style of a quarter-back in American football. To be so creative in his throwing was unusual for a goalkeeper at that time.

I should also mention Ivor Broadis, an England international who came to City from Sunderland for £25,000. I never saw Broadis play, but people whose opinion I trust spoke very highly of him.

I did, however, see Peter Broadbent from the excellent Wolves side of the late 1950s and early 1960s. I played against him in only my second game for the Manchester United first team, and at the time I thought he was a terrific player – this was just the way I saw it back then, when I was still a very young man, just eighteen or nineteen. Thinking of how I looked at the game as I got older, and the demands I would make of myself, my assessment would probably have been more rigorous if I had encountered Broadbent later on. Maybe my view of him was superficial – a bit like those people who tell me Glenn Hoddle was a great player – but I do have some support for my very high opinion of Peter Broadbent as he is also rated very highly by Big Ron Atkinson.

I was only a teenager when I saw Nat Lofthouse, the Lion of Vienna, playing for Bolton Wanderers against Manchester United in the 1958 cup final. Lofthouse scored two goals in the final, which Bolton won 2–0. He was a traditional centre-forward who was really good in the air, a strong powerful lad.

But when we get to other renowned figures of that time, such as Charlie Tully of Celtic, the picture gets a bit blurred.

Tully was a Northern Ireland lad, a left-winger who was idolised at Celtic. I was always curious about him, but I could never get a clear picture of him, even from Bobby Collins, who played with him at Celtic. When I was playing with Bobby at Leeds, I asked him about Tully and he spoke about him being able to hold the ball, and how he used to taunt the Rangers players and frustrate them with his tricks, which would obviously make him a big hit with the Celtic fans. I listened to all this stuff about the tricks and the taunts of Charlie Tully, but I still don't know how good he was.

I can, however, vouch for the credentials of Puskas, Di Stefano and Gento, stars of the Real Madrid team that won the European Cup five times in succession from its inaugural year in 1955. They played United in the semi-final in 1957, the year before Munich, and a friendship developed between the two clubs that led to a series of friendly matches, home and away. I played in two of them, in 1962 and 1963, once in Old Trafford, once in the Bernabéu, so I was able to see up close the greatness about which I had heard so much. I had been following Ferenc Puskas by reputation since as far back as 1953, when I was twelve years old and Hungary destroyed England 6–3 at Wembley. Now, at the age of twenty-one, I was playing against him, and Alfredo Di Stefano and Francisco Gento.

Technically, they were brilliant. Puskas was a chubby-looking fellow but a beautiful striker of the ball. A master player. You wouldn't see him running around much, but then you wouldn't see Kenny Dalglish running around that much either. Indeed in these days of Prozone and the like, if you compared Dalglish's stats for the amount of ground covered with those of, say, Dirk Kuyt, it's quite possible that Kenny wouldn't be in the team at all. He wouldn't even be mapped. Kenny would be doing only half the running, but somehow he'd have six times more of the ball.

It was the same with Puskas. He didn't need to cover all that ground because his positional sense was so good. As soon as the ball touched his left foot, it was immediately under control. It was, as they say, like a magic wand. He didn't score against United, but his shots were whipping past the post in a way that explained his unbelievable goal-scoring record, roughly a goal a game. He scored four in the 1960 European Cup final against Eintracht Frankfurt, when Madrid won 7–3 at Hampden Park.

Di Stefano and Puskas apparently didn't get on too well on a personal level but, as master players do, they related perfectly to each other on the pitch. Like Xavi and Iniesta, they were always of the same mind in terms of positional sense and finishing. Gento on the left wing was quick, and he had a great left foot. In fact, left-footed players always look a bit stylish on the ball, and when they happen to be Gento and Puskas, it is taken to another dimension. You can always tell when you are up against a master player. The better the technique, the closer the control, the less chance there is of them losing the ball. And above all, there is this – *after their first touch, they have more time and space than they had before they touched it.*

The more touches, the more time and space. With bad players, it works the opposite way. The more touches, the less time and space they have, and they seem to be inviting players around them.

So I can say that Puskas, Di Stefano and Gento were truly great players, and I can talk about them with a certainty that I could never fully find in the cases of Matthews and Finney.

When he was manager at Leeds, I talked to Jimmy Armfield about Stanley Matthews and Tom Finney. He was on the side of Matthews in the great debate, but he was diplomatic. He said if he was looking for an out-and-out winger, it'd be Stan. But Finney also played centre-forward and left-wing, as well as right-wing. Indeed, I remember that when I first came to England in the mid-1950s, Preston North End were having a bad time so Finney moved to centre-forward. He was brilliant there too.

Jimmy Armfield had played with Matthews at Blackpool, and this is how it generally worked out – people who played with Stan would be in favour of Stan, and people who played with Finney would be in favour of Finney. Indeed Bill Shankly, who played with Finney at Preston, spoke of him as a god.

'Tom Finney would have been great in any team, in any match, in any age ... even if he had been wearing an overcoat,' Shankly declared.

I spoke to Tommy Docherty, another former Preston man who had played at right-half behind Finney. He had no doubt. 'Finney!' he cried.

Not that Tom Finney was revered by all. When the Italian club Palermo offered him a two-year contract – which included a signing-on fee of £10,000, a monthly wage of £130, a Mediterranean villa and a continental car – he was not even allowed to consider it by his home-town club. Finney discussed the matter with the Preston chairman who allegedly told him that since he couldn't speak the language, he could hardly go off and play there, and, anyway, 'What does thee want going to Italy for, Tom?'

To the men who ran football back then, such a move suggested that a player was getting ideas above his station, and even players of the stature of Tom Finney tended to accept their fate.

The 'Bogota affair' in 1950 had taught players a harsh lesson. This was a rebellion against the maximum wage, which was £12 a week, and against conditions in general, especially the immoral system whereby there was no freedom of contract, a system which entitled the club to retain or to transfer a player entirely at their discretion. The rebellion was started by a few players – including Charlie Mitten of Manchester United,

Neil Franklin and George Mountford of Stoke City, and Billy Higgins of Everton – who received extremely attractive offers to play in Bogota in Colombia.

Mitten in particular had a keen sense of the injustice of it all, of how badly the players were being exploited in England. He wanted top professional footballers to be rewarded in the way that top professional performers of stage and screen were rewarded – in this he was ahead of his time. As part of the famous United forward line of Delaney, Pearson, Rowley, Morris and Mitten, he had been on tours to places like South America where vast crowds came to see the stars of the English game, none of whom were being paid like stars, or anything like it.

Mitten made a stand, along with the other 'Bogota' lads, but it all ended in disappointment and failure when they had to return to England after a year. The authorities made an example of them. They were fined and suspended for a year, and immediately put on the transfer list by their clubs. Mitten was transferred from United to Fulham, and he never played for England again. Neither did Franklin, though he was apparently a brilliant player, a regular international who had been regarded as the best centre-half in the country.

In the atmosphere of those times, even Tom Finney must have felt insecure – he was almost certainly the last great player who could supplement his income by plying his other trade as a plumber.

Which also tells you about the modest spirit of the man. Tommy Docherty is one of his most fervent admirers, comparing him favourably to Lionel Messi, or even the other way round: 'Lionel Messi is an immature Tom Finney. He reminds me of him with his attitude ... you never see him concerned in any tasteless things, we never hear him criticising anyone, and that was Finney. To me, Messi is Finney reborn.'

In any debate about these men, it must also be remembered that Matthews was about seven years older than Finney, and by the time the Second World War was over, which is when many of these comparisons were being made, he was thirty. Which puts him at something of a disadvantage.

I did actually see Stan playing once at Dalymount Park, in a friendly match, or what was known at the time as an 'exhibition', a game in which the two teams might be put together entirely for the one match – or it might be Bohemians playing at home at Dalymount against an English selection, all of whom were delighted to take part because they were on about £15 a week at their clubs, whereas they might get as much as £50 for an exhibition.

It must have been in the early 1950s when I saw Matthews playing in that game. There was still post-war rationing in England, and one of the great attractions of Dublin was that they could buy things in Dublin that they couldn't get in England – even for fifty quid. So the players would get the boat over, do a bit of shopping with the money they were getting for the match, and return on the boat with all sorts of fine things, such as perfume and nylons, tins of John West red salmon, and perhaps the most highly prized luxury of all, meat.

So it was that I saw the great Stanley Matthews play, and, though I was very young, I was struck by one aspect of his performance which remains with me to this day. At some stage in the second half, Matthews must have decided to turn it on. Because I recall that the full-back who was trying to stop him – an Irish international called Robin Lawler who played for Fulham – was struggling to such an extent that he was actually dizzy.

You'd often hear it said of a winger that 'he made the full-back dizzy', but it doesn't mean that the full-back is dizzy in the true sense of the word. Yet I was convinced that on that day in Dalymount, Stanley Matthews bamboozled and tormented Robin Lawler to such an extent that Lawler genuinely was dizzy. You could see Lawler approaching Matthews and he was shaking, like someone in shock.

Years later, my friend Jack Pettitt was telling me that he saw Matthews playing for England against Scotland at Wembley, a game in which, according to Jack, the Scottish left-back was given a very hard time by Stan. 'I'm not joking you, he had him dizzy,' Jack told me.

I was startled, remembering straight away that match in Dalymount. I had not told Jack about what Stan did to Robin Lawler, and yet Jack was using the same word. So that's two independent accounts of Matthews having such a traumatic effect on the full-back that they looked like they'd just been in a serious accident.

In passing, it should not be forgotten that both Matthews and Finney played their parts in the war effort – Stan joined the RAF, while Tom fought in Montgomery's Eighth Army in Egypt and later in Italy. I believe that players of that stature would not only be able to adapt to a different role in their own time, they would be able to adapt to any situation that was put in front of them. Even with the totally different pressures of today, such men would surely rise to the top. We still haven't settled that argument – Matthews or Finney? – which used to torment men like my father. To this day, there is that sense of frustration, a feeling that we should know more about them than we do. But I think we can arrive at this conclusion – the great players of their time would have been great players at any time.

2

Ramsey's Theory of Evolution

Duncan Edwards was a wing-half, a position which seems to place him in an older version of the game. The way it was, there was no back four, just the full-backs and the centre-half and these two wing-halves on the right and the left in front of them in midfield. The wing-halves would also be supporting the inside-right and the inside-left, attacking players who were expected to score at least as many goals as each other, and who made up a sort of a 'W' formation in the forward line, along with the two wingers and the centre-forward.

But because of a process of evolution, which is always going on in football, the old style of full-back was on the way out. The big cumbersome fellows, who were being destroyed by the technical brilliance and the dribbling skills of Matthews or Finney, were being replaced by a smaller, neater and much quicker kind of player, of whom the best examples would be George Cohen and Ray Wilson and our own Tony Dunne.

No more would the full-back 'dive in', making it easy for a skilful winger to go past him. In fact, the job of the winger was being made so much more difficult that a lot of people in the game were starting to think that they were better off not using the traditional sort of winger – they were just nowhere near as effective as they had been.

While they all might have been thinking it, the first man who actually did something about it was Alf Ramsey. And when he put it into practice at the 1966 World Cup with England's so-called 'wingless wonders', it seemed to surprise, and disappoint, everyone. Ramsey was blamed for diminishing the role of the winger, even though it was clear to many that they were already becoming obsolete. And with the copycat effect in football, what Ramsey did turned out to be so far-reaching you can even hear people to this day lamenting the 'wingless wonders', which in one way is very foolish – England did after all win the World Cup without wingers such as Terry Paine and John Connelly and Ian Callaghan in the latter stages – but it also gives us a sense of what a significant change this had been.

Controversial though it was, it meant that the game was developing – and for the better. After all, the sight of a big burly lad being turned inside-out and left on his backside by a nippy winger was always entertaining, but the George Cohens and the Tony Dunnes were just far better players all round, and that had to be a good thing.

If he had lived, Duncan Edwards might well have captained England to win that World Cup. He was twenty-one when he died in the Munich disaster, in 1966 he would have been in his prime. In 1955, when I joined Manchester United on a permanent basis as a boy of fifteen, I was so overawed by Edwards, and by the Busby Babes in general, that I was afraid to talk to any of them. Generally I just tried to stay out of their way. So in a strange way, though we were actually at the same club at the same time, I see Duncan Edwards as a distant figure from another time, a bit like Matthews or Finney.

He was already regarded as a great player, an England international at the age of eighteen and a member of the United team that had won the First Division twice. And while I was too young at the time to be forming mature opinions about these things, everything I have ever heard from people whose opinion I respect would suggest that Edwards was indeed a great player and that he would have gone on to achieve so much more with United and with England that he would be mentioned automatically along with Pelé and Maradona and Bobby Charlton, who has said that Edwards was the only player who made him feel inferior.

'Physically he was enormous,' Bobby recalled. 'He was strong and had a fantastic football brain. His ability was complete, right foot, left foot, long passing, short passing – he did everything instinctively.'

But as a wing-half, Edwards' role would have changed. The wing-halves were either being pushed forward into midfield or were moving back to become central defenders. At Manchester United in my time, for example, Maurice Setters had been a wing-half who moved back into the defence in the new system. At West Ham United, one of the main men who made the move back into defence was the young Bobby Moore.

The first time I saw Bobby Moore playing was when I was part of the Manchester United team that participated in a youth tournament in Switzerland. And at that stage Bobby was still a wing-half. In fact, Geoff Hurst was playing at left-half in that West Ham youth team. I was impressed by Hurst in that position but when he eventually became a centre-forward, as we know, he was one of the best in the game.

Moore, though, was the golden boy even then, soon to become the top man at West Ham. He had the skill to play at wing-half, so he was even better in the back four, where he was playing with the game in front of him. The farther you move back, the easier it is to play. Or it should be. It certainly was for Bobby. He was two-footed, and with his great control could distribute the ball brilliantly. And because he read the game so well, he was never exposed for any lack of pace.

I recall that Bobby was particularly brilliant in the 1964 FA Cup semi-final against Manchester United, which West Ham won 3–1. They went on to beat Preston North End 3–2 in the final, with a goal in the last minute by Ronnie Boyce. They also went on to win the European Cup Winners' Cup the following year, beating TSV 1860 Munich 2–0 in the final, which was also played at Wembley. And of course the year after that, Bobby, along with Martin Peters and Geoff Hurst who both scored in the final, won the World Cup.

Yet in this hugely successful period of the three Wembley victories, the year that West Ham won the FA Cup they finished fourteenth in the league, when they won the Cup Winners' Cup they finished ninth and in 1966 itself, even with these outstanding players, West Ham finished twelfth in the league.

Certainly when it was put up to Bobby on the big occasion, he responded – which is a quality that all the great players have – but I think he used to get bored. I think he found it hard to get excited about the everyday stuff of playing in a First Division that West Ham were never going to win. He seemed to need the big games, the FA Cups and the World Cups, to bring out the best of him. Because any time I played against him for Leeds, Bobby was always good but he wouldn't be driving the team. In fact, if you asked me to choose between Bobby Moore and Norman Hunter to play in the league week in, week out, I would probably pick Norman. Though for the really big game, Moore would be my man. Interestingly, I know that Norman would agree with Moore being the man you would pick for the big game.

In preferring Norman for the forty-two-match season, I could be accused of favouring him just because we were at Leeds together. But it's because I knew his qualities so well that I can speak so highly of Norman Hunter. In football, as in most other areas of life, people don't look beyond the obvious. So Norman is never mentioned these days without being called Norman 'Bites Your Legs' Hunter, which suggests that he was some sort of a Vinnie Jones-type player, just a nasty guy who couldn't actually play. He was actually an outstanding player, the best defender I ever played with. And I don't just mean that he could stop other people playing, though he could do that as well, sometimes stopping several of them at the same time. Like Bobby Moore, he could read the game really well, and with his left foot he could also deliver a pass that was completely beyond the capabilities of the likes of Vinnie Jones, or most other players for that matter. But it was his overall attitude to the game that would persuade me to actually pick him instead of Bobby Moore for playing week in, week out in the league.

Like I said, Bobby could get bored – as sometimes happens to people of special talent – but Norman was always full of enthusiasm for every game, and he made sure that everyone else shared that enthusiasm. In fact, Geoff Hurst suggested in his autobiography that Alf Ramsey had actually discussed the possibility of Norman replacing Bobby in the 1966 World Cup final itself because of his concerns that West Germany had players with the speed that could expose Bobby's lack of pace – and also because Norman played alongside Jack Charlton at Leeds, which might make them a stronger partnership.

What we know is that Norman did replace Bobby Moore in the crucial World Cup qualifier in 1973 against Poland at Wembley, after Bobby had performed poorly against Poland in the away game. And, with so much at stake, England famously drew, frustrated again and again by the crazy brilliance of goalkeeper Jan Tomaszewski, and failed to qualify for the 1974 World Cup in West Germany. And because Norman was deemed partly responsible for the Poland goal – that image of him losing possession near the touchline has been replayed a million times – he has become firmly established in the public mind as a 'bites your legs' player.

But we can look back now, all these years later, and form a

true impression of these two great players, because that is what they were. We may compare them in various ways, but we are only comparing one form of excellence with another.

Bobby Moore had that special aura about him, an air of calm authority, a presence that inspired others. He never seemed to be flustered in any way, and if he lacked pace, he turned it into a virtue by giving off this sense that he was dictating the flow of the game. Always, the top players seem to have that bit more time and space than the others, and so it was with Bobby Moore. When we think about him in the mind's eye, he is never scurrying about the place – in fact, at times he seems like the only player on the pitch, or at least the only player who is doing it right. And when we see that classic moment from the 1970 Mexico World Cup of Moore timing his tackle against Pelé perfectly, we know that we are seeing a contest between players in the same bracket – Pelé says that Moore was the best defender he ever played against. Though, again, Pelé never played against Norman Hunter.

Of course, Bobby Moore was a real London boy, just like his friend Jimmy Greaves. In fact, they were big pals, 'Mooro' and 'Greavsie', they socialised together and even played tennis together. Bobby was a keen tennis player, an all-round sportsman who had played cricket for Essex as a youth, an honour he shared with Geoff Hurst.

I read recently that Greaves really loved playing tennis, and I got the feeling that he may have loved tennis more than football – it's just that he was so good at football, and at scoring goals in particular. From the day he made his debut as an inside-right for Chelsea as a seventeen-year-old in 1957,

Jimmy had the ideal mentality to be a striker – he didn't seem to care if he missed a chance. And I don't mean that he could fool himself into thinking that it didn't matter. It was as if he really didn't give a damn. He'd say, 'Ah, fack it', and just get on with it, knowing that he probably wouldn't miss the next chance. Or the one after that. Other lads would miss a chance and they would let it get to them, not Greavsie.

All sportsmen try to strike this balance between caring and not caring. Obviously they need to care, up to a point. They need to be trying. But if they care too much, it can work against them and they just freeze. Some people can never get this balance right, others can train themselves to get it – and a rare few like Jimmy Greaves seem to be born with it.

Those of you who play golf will know that if you need to play a simple eight iron to the green to win your club championship, the pressure will just get to you, and you will probably make a mess of it, but if you're playing the same eight iron the next day, just for fun, you will be able to do it with ease.

Jimmy Greaves was always relaxed in that way, even with 40,000 people roaring at him, pleading with him to score. He was always in that laid-back frame of mind, playing that easy eight iron into the green – or in his case maybe it was more like a game of tennis, in which he was just lobbing the ball back to Bobby Moore on a Sunday morning, with nothing riding on it.

On the pitch, he sort-of played for fun. I remember going into a tackle with him, in which Greaves won the ball. But the referee gave a free kick against him. 'Facking hell, ref,' Greavsie said. 'It's the only tackle I facking won all season.' He was laughing at it.

I hasten to add that it wasn't just Greavsie's attitude that made him such a brilliant striker – he had the talent as well. In fact it was more than talent, it was genius. Any time he had a chance to score, he always looked like the odds-on favourite. And sure enough, he would just slip it into the net. I know this from personal experience, because when Greaves was put through, as a midfield player I would be running back, and I would have a good view of what he was going to do. Whatever way he went about it – whatever gift he had – when he was in a position to score, somehow he would make the goal look a mile wide, with his touch, his control, his angle of approach. When a striker is struggling, having a barren spell, lacking in confidence or ability, it is the other way round. When he is one-on-one with the goalkeeper, the goal seems to shrink, the keeper looks like a giant, and you can't imagine him scoring if he had ten or even twenty opportunities on the day.

Jimmy Greaves had very few barren spells that I can remember. His scoring record was phenomenal. In 1960, when he was only twenty, he became the youngest player to score a hundred goals in league football. A year later, he moved for a short time to play with AC Milan and he hated it, hated nearly everything about it, but he still managed to score ten goals in ten games – which was quite a feat in Italian football. Tiring quickly of the disciplinarian approach of the Italian coaches, who would make the players do things like come in for the afternoons and go away for special training, none of which were to Jimmy's liking, he came back to Tottenham Hotspur for almost £100,000. And he continued to bang them in.

He went on to score 266 goals in 379 matches for Spurs,

joining the great side that had just won the Double in 1961, and staying at Tottenham until 1970. He finished top scorer in the league on six occasions, an achievement that has never been equalled. Spurs also won the FA Cup in 1962 and 1967 during his time there and became the first English team to win a European trophy when they won the 1963 European Cup Winners' Cup, beating Atlético Madrid 5–1 in the final – and Greaves scored twice in that match too.

When he retired from top-class football in 1971, after a spell at West Ham, he had played 516 football league games and scored 357 goals, which is an all-time record. In the mid-1970s, he eventually made a comeback of sorts at a lower level, and he did what he had always done, scoring twenty-five times for Barnet in the Southern League in the 1977–1978 season. Apparently not even old age could stop Jimmy Greaves from scoring goals.

The way that Jimmy Greaves played the game would not have worked in other positions on the field. He didn't really do much in the game apart from score goals – though of course if that is your job, and you do it as well as Jimmy did, you don't really need to do much more than that. Playing with the likes of Dave Mackay and Cliff Jones in that Spurs team, Greaves only had to finish. Roy Keane, for example, would not have been much of a player if he'd had an attitude like Greavsie, which didn't involve much in the way of fierce commitment and covering every blade of grass.

But that is the way with the great players, they are not all built the same way. Sadly, it was Greaves' apparent indifference to the non-scoring aspects of the game that probably cost him his place in the later matches of the 1966 World Cup. After the team had played poorly in the first two games, Alf Ramsey felt that Geoff Hurst might contribute more to the team as a whole. But despite this misfortune, it is sometimes forgotten that Greaves was still England's main striker for the rest of the 1960s. And that he scored forty-four times in fifty-seven appearances, a better international goals-per-game ratio than even Bobby Charlton.

There was another magnificent British goal scorer who was also playing in Italy around the time that Greaves had his brief time there – John Charles. But unlike the London boy, Charles stayed in Italy for five seasons, during which he was extraordinarily successful at Juventus, and for which he is still worshipped in Turin as a god.

And what was particularly unusual about John Charles is that he was regarded as both a superb centre-forward and an outstanding centre-half. In fact, when he left his home-town team Swansea in the late 1940s at the age of seventeen to sign for Leeds United, he mostly played at centre-half. A great debate ensued about whether Charles would be better for Leeds at centre-half or centre-forward. When the Leeds manager Major Buckley eventually switched him to centre-forward in 1952 – on balance, being able to score goals is more highly valued than being able to keep them out – John Charles responded by scoring forty-two goals for Leeds in the 1953–1954 season.

Indeed Jimmy Greaves himself rated John Charles among the all-time greats in world football, probably the ultimate compliment for any goal scorer.

I believe that if John Charles was playing today, at current prices he would be worth about £100 million – and I am not exaggerating that just for effect. I think he was so prodigiously gifted, he would be valued at the most extreme end of the scale, where you find only the likes of Lionel Messi. Though, again, you could hardly imagine a player more physically different to Messi. Charles was a big, big man, with the balance and control and neatness of a little fellow, which was a terrifying prospect for any opponent. Because of his size and physique, he had an aggression that came naturally, not from any nastiness on his part. He was never booked or sent off in his career, which was a major achievement in itself when you consider all the kickings he must have taken from desperate defenders over the years – it was almost impossible to stop him by any fair means. And he was a devastating header of the ball.

When he joined Juventus in 1957, he was signed for a British record of £65,000, about double the previous record, and he was an immediate success. 'The Gentle Giant' they called him and he scored twenty-eight goals in his first season. Juventus won Serie A, and Charles was voted Player of the Year. In his five years at Juventus, Charles played 155 times and scored ninety-three goals, all against those famously tight Italian defences. In that period, Juventus won the league three times, and the Coppa Italia twice. In 1958, Charles was the Italian Player of the Year.

In fact, John Charles was so revered by the Italians that even thirty years after he left Juventus, if he walked down the streets in Turin, he would be mobbed.

The Argentinian player Sivori was another star of that

team, as was Boniperti – with Charles, Sivori and Boniperti made up the 'Magical Trio'. In fact, I once bought, and played, in an excellent pair of boots that were endorsed by Sivori. But Charles was always the main man. In 1997 Juventus fans voted him the best foreign player to have played for them, which was quite something, given that that list would have included the likes of Liam Brady and Michel Platini, as well as Sivori. Charles was also named the best foreign player ever to play in Italy, an even more remarkable tribute which placed him ahead of Diego Maradona.

Having made his debut at eighteen, Charles was a leading member of the Wales squad that went to the 1958 World Cup in Sweden, which remains the only Wales team ever to qualify for a major tournament. They remained unbeaten in the group stages and then they won a play-off against Hungary to reach the quarter-finals, where they were beaten by Brazil, the eventual winners. The decisive goal for Brazil was scored by Pelé. And John Charles was not playing that day, having been injured in the match against Hungary. It remains one of the great sadnesses of Welsh football that they were forced to play the most important match of their history without their greatest player. The Welsh manager was Jimmy Murphy, also of Manchester United, who insisted that they might well have beaten Brazil if Charles had been in the side. And knowing Murphy, he would not have made such a statement lightly.

In 1962, amid much excitement, Don Revie brought John Charles back to Leeds for a fee of £53,000, but Charles found it hard to adjust to life in England after his glorious years in Italy, and soon he was on his way back to Roma, who still regarded him highly enough to pay £70,000 for him. At this stage he was in his declining years, and ultimately returned home to Wales to play for Cardiff City.

By now, I had joined Charles' old club Leeds from Manchester United, and I played against him in Cardiff in a match in the old Second Division in 1963. He was past his best at that stage, and the new generation of Leeds players was just coming together, but whatever we achieved in the years ahead, there will always be a special place in the hearts of Leeds fans, and of all football men, for John Charles.

There is a street named after him near Elland Road, and a bust of him in what is known as the John Charles Stand. For those who were lucky enough to see him play, there are memories of a player who was not just 'a big centre-forward', but an intelligent player who knew when to glance it on, when to play a one-two that would put somebody through. And if you knocked it to the far post, he would be there.

A real footballer.

3

The Glory Game

When Dave Mackay came down from Scotland to join Tottenham Hotspur in 1959, he was an immediate sensation. This might suggest that he was a young guy bursting onto the scene at maybe eighteen years of age, but it wasn't like that.

Mackay was actually twenty-four when Spurs signed him from Hearts, his home-town club in Edinburgh. And they paid just over £30,000 for him, which wasn't a huge amount of money for a player already well established in Scotland – and which turned out to be a very small amount of money when it became clear what Mackay could do.

It has always been a bit of a mystery to me why Mackay wasn't signed earlier in his career by one of the big English clubs. The Hearts team that he captained, managed by Tommy Walker and featuring players such as Alex Young and Alfie Conn, had been hugely successful. In the late 1950s Mackay had won the league, the Scottish Cup and the League Cup with them, and had been the captain in the 1957–1958 season when Hearts scored 152 league goals and conceded only twenty-nine, a British record.

I refer again to my friend Jack Pettitt, who remembers Hearts coming down to play friendlies against Aston Villa two or three times in those years, and that he couldn't understand why Villa didn't sign Dave Mackay at that time. According to Jack, Mackay was always brilliant.

So why didn't they sign him?

Eventually I asked the man himself, when we got talking on the sad occasion of the funeral of Billy Bremner in 1997. Billy, of course, was my midfield partner at Leeds for years, but he and Dave also had a bit of history – which can be seen in that very funny photograph of Mackay grabbing Billy by the front of his shirt during a match between Spurs and Leeds in 1966, a game in which I played. Mackay appears to be trying to lift the smaller man off the ground as he glares at him furiously. There is something about the helpless expression on Billy's face and the rage on Mackay's that is straight out of a cartoon. The official version goes that Billy was pleading his innocence after a late tackle on Mackay, who was supposedly infuriated because he had just come back from a second broken leg. But my take on it would be slightly different. Dave was a real tough nut, and even if he had been bothered about getting his leg broken again, he would never have admitted it. I don't think that was really the source of his anger. There had been some sort of a clash between them on the pitch, but Dave's reaction was that of a man who resented Billy for deeper reasons. Dave only had twenty-two Scottish caps, mainly because the system was a mess. And Billy was now captain of Scotland, a much younger man who already had more caps than Dave. Like a lot of great players, Mackay was a bit of a bully. And as he grabbed Billy by the shirt, if we could put his actions into words, I think they would go something like this: 'I'm a better player than you ever were, you little shit.' Dave would have been an idol to Billy, and Billy's attitude is, 'I didn't mean it, Dave.' Which only makes him seem like more of a little shit to Dave.

So as we paid our respects to Billy and talked about old times, I asked Dave for his own opinion about why it took so long for a big English club to sign him, and he suggested that it might have been something to do with an injury issue. Matt Busby had definitely been interested in signing him for Manchester United, because Busby had also been manager of Scotland, so he knew how good Mackay was. But then Mackay had broken a bone in his foot and was out for a while. When he returned, he broke a bone in his foot again, at which point he guessed that Busby must have got scared and decided not to take the chance.

Which turned out to be a big mistake on Busby's part. Because Bill Nicholson eventually signed him for Spurs, and Mackay transformed them. In fact, I played against them in my league debut for Manchester United in September 1959, and that Spurs team of Mackay and Danny Blanchflower, Cliff Jones and Tommy Harmer 'The Charmer' beat us 5–1 at Old Trafford. They should have won the league that season, but they managed to blow it with a bad run of results around Easter. As if to erase that completely from their memories, the next season they did the unthinkable, winning the league and then beating Leicester City in the FA Cup final, becoming the first club to do the Double in the twentieth century.

Mackay was a wing-half, but he didn't stick to his position. As I've said, around this time there was a move away from the old system, in which everybody had his place, and certainly no fixed position could contain the abilities of Dave Mackay. At Fulham, Johnny Haynes was starting to go wherever the ball was, rather than waiting for it to come to him. He was dictating the play, rather than just sticking to the old inside-forward role. At Spurs, Mackay was doing something similar, but not in a constructive way like Haynes. Mackay's genius was for destruction.

He would tackle anyone. If I was playing on the right wing, and I held on to it long enough, he would be there tackling me. If Bobby Charlton on the left wing held on to it long enough, Mackay would be tackling him. He was full of energy, full of devilment, full of go. He couldn't half win the ball – and when he had won it, he couldn't half play. As he proved towards the end of his career when he played at the back for Derby County, he was a wonderful distributor of the ball. And Brian Clough, who along with Peter Taylor signed him for Derby, eventually described him as the greatest player that Spurs had ever had – he didn't say that too loudly in 1968, when he signed Mackay for about £5,000. Admittedly Mackay was thirty-three at the time, but it was a masterstroke by Clough and Taylor, and

Mackay proceeded to lead Derby out of the Second Division and be named Footballer of the Year jointly with Tony Book of Manchester City.

It was those glory days at Tottenham though that established Dave Mackay beyond any doubt as a great player. Not only did they win the Double in 1960–1961, they did it in style, setting a record by winning their first eleven league games and eventually winning the league by eight points. They won the FA Cup again the following year, beating Burnley in the final, and just missed out on a repeat of the Double when they finished a close third in the league behind Ipswich Town and Burnley. They went on to beat Atlético Madrid in the final of European Cup Winners' Cup in 1963, and they won the FA Cup again in 1967, beating Chelsea 2–1 in what was called the Cockney Cup final, because it was the first to feature two London teams.

Spurs also had the Welsh international Cliff Jones playing on the left or the right wing. An outstanding player, Jones was a great raider, who scored a lot of goals coming in from the wing – a role for which you had to be technically good and really brave. Jones was exceptionally brave. He was also exceptionally quick. He was only a smallish guy, but he had a good heart and he could really go. Wingers are supposed to be easy targets, a bit soft, but Cliff would give as good as he got at any time. A real top-notcher.

If Mackay was the dynamo for Spurs, the captain Danny Blanchflower gave leadership in all sorts of other ways. Because people always like the easy labels, they tended to see Dave as the tank and Danny as the classy right-half – but it was a bit more complicated than that. In fact, Danny himself would no doubt have dismissed such labels, because he was an original thinker who would never just state the obvious.

Blanchflower had been part of my childhood, when I was following the game from afar in Dublin. I was only about nine years of age when he was transferred from Glentoran in Belfast to Barnsley for £6,000. And I was eleven when Aston Villa bought him for £15,000, little thinking that one day in the not-too-distant future I would be shaking hands with him after playing my first game for Manchester United. Apparently he grew tired of the primitive training methods at Villa, which involved almost no practice with the ball, only physical exercise, and with the game changing all around them, Blanchflower felt that Villa were falling behind. In 1954, when he was twenty-eight, Spurs bought him for the enormous sum of £30,000.

I had also followed his career as captain of the Northern Ireland team that contained his brother Jackie, a Manchester United player, and which reached the quarter-final of the 1958 World Cup in Sweden. Like Wales, they were knocked out at that stage, but they had got further in the tournament than both England and Scotland.

Danny was inspirational, and not just as a player. He was inspirational in his approach to everything. 'Football is about glory.' he said. 'It is about doing things in style and with a flourish, about going out and beating the lot, not waiting for them to die of boredom.' He was articulate, and he used his way with words to challenge the manager if necessary. Cliff Jones, Dave Mackay and the other Spurs players loved him. They saw Danny as a real leader, maybe not quite in the same class as Mackay as a player, but always able to make a skilful contribution. When the team was attacking, he'd move to the right wing to be in a good position to receive the ball. With his excellent positional sense all round, and his passing, he was always a creative force. In fact he was always thinking about the game, and on the train home from a match Danny would 'have the salt and pepper out', as we say, to analyse the game and to explain some discovery he had made.

Probably if I had to choose between two Dave Mackays and two Danny Blanchflowers, I would eventually choose the two Dave Mackays. But I am happy that I will never have such a dilemma. And Blanchflower was such an original thinker, maybe that was the vital ingredient that drove Spurs to the Double, to imagine that they could do it when no one else thought they could, to break through that mental barrier.

I got to know Danny when I was player-manager at West Bromwich Albion and, in any conversation I had with him, it was clear that he was the sort of man who thought outside the box. Way outside the box.

By then, he had a column in the *Sunday Express* which always had that stamp of the intellectual about it, the urge to challenge authority. He told me that it was he who had introduced the idea of the wall for free kicks. I would not doubt it. He also told me that we had almost become colleagues at Tottenham. When Bill Nicholson was retiring as manager, Bill had wanted Danny to take his place. But he had also envisaged a role for me, given that I was in my thirties and presumed to be interested in a career in coaching or management when I eventually stopped playing. The idea was that, with Danny as manager, I would be a sort of a coach on the pitch. And Danny explained in some detail how this Spurs team of ours would have played without a centre-forward. Which was a bit off-the-wall, admittedly, but I didn't say that to Danny at the time. He was very convincing. I listened, knowing it would never have happened – in the area of management, I would either do it myself or not do it at all.

Anyway, the Spurs job went to Terry Neill. Probably the Spurs directors just couldn't cope with the thought of having to deal with Danny and his refusal to take any nonsense, his determination to do things his way. This was the man, after all, who had been selected as a subject for *This Is Your Life* and who had walked away from it. Danny Blanchflower became the first man ever to turn down Eamonn Andrews.

For younger readers, it is hard to explain just how outrageous this seemed, except to say that it was a bit like someone being awarded an Oscar and refusing to accept it. At the time, if Eamonn Andrews approached anyone with his big red book containing the life story of the person who had been chosen, it was considered one of the greatest honours you could get in Britain, a bit like getting a knighthood. And the show had a huge audience, partly because of the element of surprise, the fact that the recipients of the honour didn't know that this was going to happen until the last moment. They might be under the impression that they were in the studio for some other programme entirely, set up by people telling them all sorts of lies about the real purpose of the event. And then Eamonn Andrews would suddenly appear, putting his arm around them as he broke the news.

Great news it usually was, for anyone in public life. Anyone, that is, except Danny Blanchflower, who felt that it was an invasion of privacy. And while you couldn't help but admire him for being so independent, you knew that that is probably what Danny Blanchflower would be mainly remembered for by the general public, not the fact that he made such a brilliant contribution to the game of football. Mind you, he wasn't against television in general by any means. He may have spoiled everything for *This Is Your Life* but when the call came he was happy to be a guest on *Parkinson*. That was more Danny's style.

You would never expect Dave Mackay to be involved in any controversy in the area of showbusiness, and then *The Damned United* came along. Because most of the attention has been focused on the portrayal of the Leeds players, incuding myself, in the book and the film, not as much attention has been paid to the equally poor treatment of Dave Mackay. I had problems with the book, and I took a successful legal action against it. In Dave's case, it was the film that misrepresented him, by suggesting that he had broken a strike organised by the Derby County players to have Brian Clough reinstated as manager. In fact, Mackay wasn't even at Derby at the time, having already left to become player-manager at Swindon Town in 1971.

Why the film's makers felt free to tarnish the reputation of a great player in that way is totally beyond me. Dave was successful in his legal action, though, like the rest of us, he could have done without it.

The combination of Blanchflower from Northern Ireland

and Mackay from Scotland seemed to be more than the sum of its parts. The Scottish inside-right John White, or 'The Ghost', also made a major contribution to that Tottenham team. He was a very, very skilful player who was tragically killed by lightning on a golf course in 1964.

And it seemed in general that successful teams needed this Scottish or Irish element. George Best from Northern Ireland, Denis Law from Scotland and Bobby Charlton of England was probably the most perfect combination at Manchester United. And it is hard to imagine the great Liverpool teams without the Scottish and Irish elements of Ian St John, Graeme Souness, Ronnie Whelan and Kenny Dalglish. I'd also have to say that the Leeds team with Billy Bremner, Eddie Gray and Peter Lorimer from Scotland and myself from Dublin had the right chemistry.

It seems to be the case, too, that when we are talking about the great teams, we mainly talk about the midfield players rather than, say, the full-backs. Even the really good ones, like Shay Brennan and Tony Dunne at United, are seen as auxiliaries, rather than the men who make it happen.

But you have to be very lucky to get all the combinations right, and in some cases there is no combination at all, it is mainly left down to one man. At Fulham in the late 1950s and early 1960s that man was Johnny Haynes. While Mackay and Blanchflower were changing the game and winning trophies at Tottenham, Haynes was doing his own bit to change the game – though the Fulham team that he captained never won a trophy.

At the time, I was a young player at United, and what Haynes was doing was a revelation to me. The way that he cast aside the old restrictions and got into a better position than anyone else to receive the ball – he wasn't waiting for it, he was making the ball come to him. I saw him playing, both as a spectator and an opponent – in fact my first goal for United was scored at Fulham – and I could see that he was a great passer, with wonderful technique. Maybe he wasn't quite one of the kill-your-granny-to-win brigade, but Haynes was beautifully gifted. And if he lacked that killer instinct of a Dave Mackay or a Bobby Collins, it has to be said that the London lads in general tended to have a slightly different attitude to these things. I suppose you could call it a broader view of life, maybe a bit more relaxed than the lads from the north or the lads from Scotland or even some of the Irish lads – 'What's the facking problem?', as Jimmy Greaves might say in his easy-osy style, if things were getting a bit too intense.

In fact, in the early 1970s I got to know Johnny Haynes slightly when we played a few rounds of golf together, and I found him to be very friendly, but quite a reserved type of lad. We never really got talking about football, and I didn't feel free to ask him about various aspects of his career. Because as my own career developed as I got older – and given that I was playing in a Leeds team that was always looking to win the title – my view of Haynes got a bit more complicated. Fulham might have a good run in the FA Cup, but in the league they were never any more than a good mid-table team, which meant that Haynes never played in those eight or nine games at the end of the season when things get tight and you really have to perform.

The game in general was getting more pressurised, with a

team like Spurs now expected to do well in Europe as well as everything else. In fact, Spurs were supposed to be interested at one point in signing Haynes. And while he was tied to a contract like every other player at the time, we don't know if he made any great effort to get away from Fulham. Personally, I'd love to have seen him demand a move.

Maybe he did, and it just didn't happen. All we know for sure is that he remained a one-club man, probably because he was comfortable with it. He would become the first player to get £100 a week, which probably made him even more comfortable. In fact it is no exaggeration to say that at Fulham he was a god. And as a result, we never got to see this brilliant player under real pressure, either with his club or with England. At the time the national team was something of a shambles – until, that is, they got serious for the 1966 World Cup. Up to that point, England had been managed by men like Walter Winterbottom, and there was a Selection Committee, so we need hardly add that they kept flopping in major competitions and never had a good run. When they were beaten by Brazil in the quarter-final of the 1962 World Cup in Chile, Alf Ramsey took over from Winterbottom. And because of circumstances beyond Ramsey's control, Haynes was never picked for England again. He was in a car accident in 1962, in which he sustained leg injuries including one to his knee which was serious enough to keep him out of the game for a season. And he was clearly not the same player after that.

There has been much debate about whether or not Ramsey would have picked Haynes for the World Cup squad if he'd still been at the peak of his powers – Haynes was thirty-one in

1966. I think that Ramsey would have picked him. Of course he was an 'individual' sort of player, but that doesn't mean he was Rodney Marsh. He was a real player, and I think that Ramsey would have embraced him. But it was not to be. I would have loved to see Johnny Haynes performing under that most intense pressure of a World Cup semi-final or final. But he remains a really important figure, both in the development of the game in England and in my own development as a player. For that I will always hold him in the highest regard.

4

Great Expectations

I was starting out as a full-time professional at a time of growing ambition in the game in general. In the early 1960s, the European competitions were becoming more important all the time, but it took a while for the English sides to adjust. That outstanding Spurs team did reach the semi-final of the European Cup in 1962, where they were beaten on aggregate by Benfica, but you still had this sense of a game in transition from the old days when supporters would go along to 'enjoy the match', to this newer version in which they might enjoy the match but the result would have to be right too.

And if the opponent was Benfica or Real Madrid or Budapest Honvéd or Dynamo Moscow, it could be a bit of a shock to the system. English pride was hurt by those heavy defeats to Hungary in the early 1950s, but at least there was a bit more thinking about the game. Wolves, for example, who were a very good side in the late 1950s managed by Stan Cullis, played friendly matches against some of these top European sides under floodlights – still a rare enough sight at the time. And there were huge crowds at these matches, generating levels of interest and money that were bound to encourage others to adopt a progressive approach.

Matt Busby had led the way in this regard. But in these changing times, Wolves and Burnley, the league winners, did not perform well in the European Cup. Continental football was still ahead in many ways, not least the amount of money the players received, especially in Spain and Italy – fortunes by comparison with the top English players who had lived for so long under the regime of the maximum wage. The Real Madrid side that won the European Cup five times had become an established team before the English clubs had even entered the competition. The fifth time Real Madrid won it, in 1960 at Hampden Park – when they famously beat Eintracht Frankfurt 7–3 – that team of Di Stefano and Puskas and Gento was described by the TV commentator as 'the greatest club side the world has ever known'.

Television coverage had made it all look very glamorous, and Madrid had given a great exhibition. So, in England, winning the league had suddenly become a much bigger deal because it offered the possibility of all the glamour, riches and glory at the end of it. Players could no longer feel as comfortable about finishing in fifth or sixth in the league, because there was a new European competition for teams that finished second, third and fourth in their leagues, the Fairs Cup – and it would become a really tough competition, harder to win in some ways than the European Cup itself.

And there was also the European Cup Winners' Cup, the least of the three competitions but the one in which the English teams did well straight away. Tottenham won it in 1963, becoming the first English team to win a European trophy of any kind. And West Ham won it in 1965. And while these were real achievements, it must be remembered that the cup competitions in other countries were not treated as seriously as the FA Cup was in England. In fact, there was no comparison between the cup in, say, Romania and the English equivalent, which was still such a huge prize.

It would remain a huge prize for about the next twenty years, but there was no doubt that the structures of the game had shifted, and the league was now really important as well. The end of the maximun wage in 1961 also meant that certain teams who had been very prominent in the English game started to fade – at clubs like Burnley, Blackburn, Bolton and Blackpool, players were not as content as they had been when they were actually doing better financially than the players at London clubs because it was cheaper to live in the north.

Of course, Matt Busby had been a major influence behind these steps forward, but in the early 1960s another great figure emerged to challenge him. When Bill Shankly became manager of Liverpool in 1959, his record in management had not been spectacular. He had been at places like Carlisle, Grimsby, Workington and Huddersfield, and no team of his had finished higher than mid-table in the Second Division. Based on results alone, it is hard to know what made the directors of Liverpool seek him out, though it should be remembered that at the time Liverpool were actually below Shankly's Huddersfield Town in the Second Division. He also had a reputation for developing players such as Ray Wilson and Denis Law, and he had a magnetic personality, that strange thing known as charisma.

There are always individuals who have a club that is made for them, and Shankly and Liverpool were made for each other. I never saw Bill Shankly play for Preston North End, but I imagine he must have been an all-action, enthusiastic type. He was football crazy, full of drive and energy that he was able to pass on to the players at Liverpool, and he had a way of relating to the fans that was completely genuine. Ian St John told me that when the players went along to the supporters' functions, everyone including the players would be singing 'You'll Never Walk Alone', but that the players, who were not the most natural singers, might be a bit embarrassed – not Shankly though, who would be belting it out, believing every word of it.

Of the many stories about Shankly's obsession with the game, one of my favourites is the one where he was asked if it was true that he had brought his wife Nessie to watch Rochdale playing at home, in order to celebrate their wedding anniversary. Shankly was shocked to the core at the suggestion – 'Naaah,' he said dismissively. 'I'd never get married during the football season.' And then he added, 'It was to celebrate her birthday.' And there was one other thing: 'It wasn't Rochdale. It was Rochdale Reserves.'

It certainly puts into perspective some of the more family-friendly aspects of the modern game, like the way that some players might declare themselves unavailable for an important match in order to be present at the birth of their child. When I hear that sort of talk, I wonder what Shankly would have made of it. And I shudder.

Even with the surge in the game's finances, with Shankly it wasn't about money, it was about the glory. I played for Manchester United against his Liverpool team in the 1962–1963 season when they came up to the First Division, and they played with a drive that mirrored that of Shankly, a drive I hadn't seen before. Like all the great managers, Shankly had weeded out a lot of players who didn't have that quality, and found a few who did.

Tottenham had some of that drive, and a lot of class, but with Dave Mackay breaking his leg and with Blanchflower getting older and then the death of John White, they had started to look ordinary. Certainly next to that Liverpool team and to the Manchester United team that became Liverpool's main rivals over the next few years, they were in decline. The players who won the league for Liverpool in 1963–1964 and 1965–1966 were becoming established.

Ian St John was a really top-class player, who wore number nine but who also played deep, not unlike an early version of Kenny Dalglish. He could create goals and he could score them, and he was great in the air. Ian also had the sort of personality that reflected the attitude of his manager. He was a cocky lad, Scottish too, and he wasn't afraid of winning. The Saint would not be troubled by doubts during the run-in. He was very sound technically, but he also had a good knowledge of the game on the pitch. With his excellent temperament, he could keep his head under pressure – some lads can do it better than others. Ian would have been one of the real leaders in the dressing room. Shankly had a lot of good lads at Liverpool, but they needed the extra confidence that Ian St John could bring to them.

On Merseyside, they were always making the comparison between St John at Liverpool and Alex Young at Everton. Young was another Scot, known as the 'Golden Vision', a name given to him by Danny Blanchflower, who said that Young represented 'the view every Saturday that we have of a perfect world, a world that has got a pattern and is finite. And that's Alex – the Golden Vision.' And indeed Young had made his name with an outstanding Hearts team which also produced Blanchflower's colleague at Spurs, Dave Mackay. Signed by Everton for over £40,000, Young was a member of the team managed by Harry Catterick that won the league in 1962–1963, just before Liverpool really got going. There was Young, Jimmy Gabriel, Roy Vernon, Johnny Morrissey, Brian Labone and Ray Wilson, and though they won the cup in 1966, they did not dominate as Liverpool would. Young was always idolised by the Everton fans, for the way he seemed to glide across the muddy pitches and, in 1969, the film-maker Ken Loach made a drama documentary about him called *The Golden Vision*, which was shown as part of the famous 'Play For Today' series on the BBC. Young was an attractive player – Jimmy Greaves called him 'Nureyev on grass' – but I always thought there was more substance to Ian St John.

Ian Callaghan was also a real player. He gave tremendous service to Liverpool on the right wing and later in midfield well into the 1970s. I particularly remember him for the fact that in the 1965 FA Cup final against Leeds he delivered the cross in the second period of extra time that Ian St John headed in, with all that confidence of his, to beat us 2–1. To tell the truth, Leeds were still a work in progress at the time, and Liverpool were much better than us on the day. Any time we played them during those years, they had that great will to win, they really wanted to do it. The other goal in extra time that won the cup in 1965 was scored by Roger Hunt, a top player, a terrific lad, and a really good character who did it when it mattered. He eventually scored almost 250 goals for Liverpool and, like Callaghan, was as honest as the day is long.

Peter Thompson on the wing for Liverpool was another who probably looked more attractive on the ball than St John, but who was not as effective. Willie Stevenson was a good footballer. There was Gordon Milne, who was one of Shankly's first signings – Shankly had played at Preston North End with Gordon's father, Jimmy. Gordon suffered with injuries, which probably meant that Shankly would simply ignore him for long periods, totally unsympathetic to a player who was of no use to him – some have always thought this a funny trait of Shankly's, I always thought it was pretty horrible.

But he was never disappointed by Chris Lawler. Chris was a very quiet lad who never missed a match and who scored an amazing number of goals from full-back, another top-class player. Ron Yeats and Tommy Smith didn't spend too much time on the treatment table either, unlike quite a few of their opponents. They were hard nuts. Ron was a good stopper, signed by Shankly from Dundee United and made captain. Tommy would take your head off, but he could also play. Throughout the team, there was this great honesty of effort, a sense of a powerful unit playing with pace and tempo and doing it for a set of supporters who identified with them – and the manager – totally.

I never found Shankly great technically, but he made up for it in other ways, with power and passion and optimism. I also now believe that about 90 per cent of management is about bringing the right players to the club, with the right character. In 1967, Shankly brought in Emlyn Hughes from Blackpool for £65,000. Emlyn would have appealed to him, right to the core of his being. He had that spirit that Shankly wanted, always aware of the need to create the right environment at the club, and to maintain it. However, it wasn't until the arrival of Graeme Souness in 1978 that Liverpool had a genuinely creative midfield player, and that was after Shankly had left. But they had other attributes, and they believed in what they were doing, pumped up by Shankly telling them how great they were and how useless the opposition were – when West Ham, with Moore, Peters and Hurst, played at Anfield, Shankly would tell his players that he'd seen the London lads 'coming in red-eyed, they've been on the piss all night'.

By the time he was done, Shankly had created more than a team, he had founded a religion. Man for man, his team may not have been as talented at the time as Manchester United's, but they did it, and they would keep on doing it for the next few years. When they made the breakthrough, winning the league in 1963–1964, it was up to United in particular to match them. And as it turned out, they would do a bit more than that. Shankly didn't believe in superstars. But that is not to say that if he'd had the choice, he wouldn't have had George Best or Denis Law in his team.

For the past forty years or so, whenever there is talk about the great players, eventually it comes down to a select few who are generally regarded as the greatest of them all. And George Best is always in that elite group, along with Pelé, Cruyff, Maradona and now Messi. Again, Bobby Charlton is usually absent, which is interesting. So is Dave Mackay. And Kenny Dalglish might be overlooked. And John Robertson is always overlooked. But most of the time, after much consideration, George tends to be given the verdict over Pelé by a fraction, perhaps influenced by a quotation attributed to Pelé that he regarded George as the greatest.

George himself, on the talk shows or in his career in showbusiness in general, never discouraged that kind of talk, but deep down I'm sure he knew there was something basically wrong with it. George was a highly intelligent lad, and he knew that greatness in football, or indeed in any walk of life, was about more than just talent, even if the talent in question was one of the most amazing the world had ever seen. He also knew that the great players, if they can stay fit, tend to be reaching their peak around the age of twenty-nine – but by the time George was twenty-six he had already retired from the game to all intents and purposes.

So what we have with George is a phenomenon. He was the first of his type to come along, and he remains the only one of his type. I was in the process of leaving Manchester United when George was starting to make his mark and, within a couple of months he was one of the most famous men in the world, a huge star. Not a star as Matthews or Finney had been, he was a new kind of star. There has been enough written about George'e lifestyle at this stage, and I do not wish to add to it. I don't care about that stuff in itself, only in the sense that it eventually took over from the football, and turned George from a genius into a victim.

George Best was maybe the most talented player I have come across. In the way he would do certain things – things I have never seen anyone else do in all my time in the game – he was uniquely gifted. For example, I never saw anyone who was as well balanced on both sides. Even Lionel Messi, who is so gifted, does it off his left side. Messi, when he is running at full pelt, can pull it back with the inside of his left foot. George could do it off both sides, running at full pelt. George was very quick and strong. He was also brave. Outside the game, he might have had no protection from his own success, but on the pitch he could ride the tackles of defenders like Ron Harris who did everything they could to kick him, but still somehow failed to stop him from scoring. And he would be doing this on the muddy pitches of the 1960s.

Ron Harris couldn't take George down, but showbusiness could, and did. On the talk shows they're always showing his goal in extra time in the 1968 European Cup final, when he rounded the Benfica keeper and scored. There is a suggestion that George was at his peak at that time, but I think he had gone a bit showbiz already. On a couple of other occasions earlier in that final, in normal time, George was through with United players on either side of him. In those moments, Pelé would have released the ball, so would Cruyff. In fact one of the reasons that Pelé was such a great player was because he always did the simple thing, when that was the right thing to do. With Messi too, if the simple ball is on, he will play it. You don't really appreciate true greatness just by seeing video clips of all the spectacular stuff. In fact, most footballers can probably put together a pretty good video of themselves doing all sorts of exciting things, but that is not the point. George didn't need any of it. He didn't need to go showbiz, to be thinking, 'I'll show everyone how good I am.' But even on his most glorious night at Wembley in 1968, you could see it starting to happen.

It was not always like that. In the earlier part of his career, George had been just as professional as Denis Law and Bobby Charlton, who were always good pros. United did after all win the league in 1964–1965 and again in 1966–1967, sharing the four titles with Liverpool in four years. From what I knew about that famous partnership of Best, Law and Charlton, I never got the impession that those three guys would be talking tactics among themselves – they went their separate ways on a personal level – but that just shows how professional they were. When something needed to be done on the pitch, they did it.

George may have succumbed to the appalling pressures he was under, but throughout their careers I never saw Denis Law or Bobby Charlton going out of their way to show off. Which is the ultimate in professionalism. In fact, Denis didn't have a great reputation for being able to do what they call 'keepy-uppy'. You can see street performers with special skills in that area who can keep the ball in the air for a lot longer than Denis Law could, and people are throwing pennies at them. Denis, who couldn't do that stuff, was still signed by United from Torino for a British record of £115,000 and became European Footballer of the Year in 1964–1965. Then again, on the pitch in a real game, how many times do you see a player doing 'keepy-uppies'? It's actually not part of the game at all, it's just a circus act. Not that I would discourage kids from doing it. There's no harm in it, and it is good for them to practise with the ball.

Denis Law didn't have that particular skill, but what he did have was that essential thing – his first touch was very good. Again we are back at basic principles. With your first touch, you control the ball, which gives you more time and space to play. The more touches, the more time and space. All the great players have this, and Denis had it to a very high degree, at speed, in competitive matches. I was with Denis for about a year at United, after his move from Italy, and I never heard him talk much about the game. He was just a great talent, who went out there and did it. He was a good header of the ball and reasonable on both sides, but the main thing about Denis was that he was the most dynamic player I have ever seen, and I'd include everyone in that, be they English, Irish, Italian or Spanish.

Denis did not have a great shot – he rarely scored from outside the box – but he had this natural urgency and aggression which meant that if the ball broke loose, he would be the first onto it, smacking it into the back of the net. With his quick reflexes, he could not be stopped. If he was going to head it, he'd do that too, into the back of the net.

Sadly he lost some of that urgency when a knee injury, which was not properly diagnosed or treated, lingered on. And Denis without his urgency was like Samson getting his hair cut. The injury kept him out of the 1968 European Cup final, and though he played on after that, he never quite recaptured that dynamism which had distinguished him. He was still good, it's just that he had become a mortal.

But even during his immortal years, Denis would have acknowledged that three players – even three players as good as himself, Charlton and Best – don't make a good team. You need men like Pat Crerand and Nobby Stiles, who of course was a huge influence in those years, doing all the right things without the glamour. Nobby would also have a major influence on the career of Eusebio, another player who was up there with the greats – though Eusebio could have done without Nobby's influence.

Eusebio was a terrific player, very quick, with a great shot in his right foot. He was also regarded as one of the gentlemen of the game, always prepared to acknowledge the good play of an opponent. But Nobby marked him so diligently in the 1966 World Cup semi-final it was said that he 'left his mark' on Eusebio. They came up against each another again in the 1968 European Cup final, when Eusebio seemed certain to score the winner for Benfica in the last minute, running into the box and blasting a shot which was stopped and held magnificently by Alex Stepney. Eusebio was as amazed as everyone else by the save, and he applauded Stepney, another of the less celebrated players of that United team. The Irish internationals Shay Brennan and Tony Dunne at full-back were also top-class players, even if they are generally seen as background figures behind the big three.

Perhaps that United team had a bit of extra class that Liverpool didn't have, but then Liverpool had the extra drive. After 1968, United started to decline, what with Law's knee not getting any better and George messing about, and nobody of their stature coming through to replace them. And Liverpool were getting past their best too – Ian St John was still good, but they weren't winning any more. Manchester City were coming on, and so were Chelsea and Leeds United, to break the dominance of Manchester United and Liverpool.

But those two sides, and those great players, had raised the game for everyone.

5

The Could-Have-Beens, the Should-Have-Beens and the Really-Weres

When Manchester City were on their way to winning the Premier League in 2012, we started to see a lot of attention being paid to Mike Summerbee, Francis Lee, Tony Book and the rest of the City team that last won the league for the club in 1967–1968. Like the 2012 City team, they had taken over from Manchester United as the champions, but unlike them they had done it without the investment of hundreds of millions or its equivalent, just those essential ingredients that had brought such success to United and Liverpool – the discovery and the development of outstanding young players, a few astute signings and inspirational management.

Joe Mercer had played for Everton and Arsenal before going on to manage Sheffield United and Aston Villa. He had had some bad injuries as a player and some health problems in general that he had overcome by the time he was made manager of City in 1965. In fact, you would not know he had ever endured these setbacks because Mercer always seemed to have a sunny disposition – his biography was called *Football with a Smile*.

But there wasn't much to smile about in 1965, when City were in the Second Divison where they had been for a couple of years, doing nothing. But things were about to change, partly with the arrival of Joe Mercer, but mainly because of the arrival of the man brought in by Joe Mercer as his assistant manager, Malcolm Allison. Not only were City about to be transformed, the game itself was about to hit another turning point.

Managers such as Bill Shankly, Matt Busby, Harry Catterick and Alf Ramsey had been very well known in a certain way, but they were not high profile in the Malcolm Allison sense. To the general public, the game was still mainly about the players. But Allison promoted the culture of the coach and the manager in a way it had never been done before. You could not imagine Ramsey smoking big cigars and drinking champagne, and you could not imagine Shankly having his picture taken in the team bath with the soft porn star Fiona Richmond as Malcolm Allison did, an incident for which Malcolm would be charged by the FA for bringing the game into disrepute.

But that was in 1976, with Crystal Palace, when Malcolm was on the way down. When he was on the way up from the Second Division with City, he was a bit more grounded, and he was brilliant. By the time he was finished in football, I'm not sure if he had done a great deal for the game in general, with all his self-promotion. The cult of the coach led to a lot of people, many of them not really football men at all, taking their coaching 'badges'. Indeed it was becoming a necessity. And the effects of this are still with us today, when even the coach of an under-12 team wants to be a winning coach, often to the detriment of the more creative kids who will be tempted to try things which may put the 'big game' in the under-12 league at risk. Malcolm Allison was certainly not one of those coaches, but, with his charisma and his success at City, he helped to create that culture in which the coach had become the man. Indeed it is putting it mildly to say that he was successful at City, because the first time around at Maine Road, along with Mercer, he revolutionised the club. The combination of the two men seemed to work perfectly, with Joe acting as the go-between with the board, and Malcolm in charge of team matters.

Allison had been interested in coaching when he was a player at West Ham, where he exchanged ideas about the game with the likes of Dave Sexton, Frank O'Farrell, John Bond and Noel Cantwell. Forced into retirement by tuberculosis, he coached in non-league football and then with Plymouth Argyle, with whom he actually reached a League Cup semi-final before a dispute with the board led to his dismissal in 1965.

At City, he found a number of young players such as Glyn Pardoe, Alan Oakes, Mike Doyle and Neil Young, the quieter types who are not as well remembered as Mike Summerbee, Francis Lee, Colin Bell and Tony Book. And like the Liverpool team under Shankly, they knitted together. Malcolm had been to the continent to have a look at training methods, a move that was most unusual back then. In that, he was ahead of his time. He got the players fit, he encouraged them to get out and play, and he convinced them they were better than any opposition.

Anything I have heard about Allison from those who played under him has been good. They loved him, and they believed in him. Mike Summerbee was quoted as saying, 'Malcolm changed football by making us train like athletes. He also knew the game inside out and could change a game without writing it down on a piece of paper. He was one of the lads, but he knew how to crack the whip and we all respected him. He had a wonderful character, and my wife always said, "You love Malcolm Allison more than you love me."'

There is also an interesting comment that I saw in *Backpass* magazine by a UEFA fitness and conditioning coach called Roger Spry, which places Malcolm Allison in a broader context in the history of the game:

In one sense he was a fraud in that he was this flamboyant character to the media and the public, but in private he was quiet and dedicated, and one of the most knowledgable coaches I have worked with. I have worked with some of the best in the business, including José Mourinho and Arsène Wenger, and I would put Malcolm in that category. José worked with Malcolm at Vitória Setúbal [where Allison was manager in the late 1980s], and I can see Malcolm in him in 90 per cent of the things he does. Malcolm was a luminary and a visionary.

But Allison had the players too, and we don't want to make the usual mistake of understating just how good those players were. Mike Summerbee was a right-winger who swapped positions a bit with Franny Lee at centre-forward. He could make goals and he could score goals and he could really play. Maybe he and Franny Lee were not everyone's favourites because they were very aggressive, and this may have put them a bit behind the magical trio of Best, Charlton and Law in the public affections – though Denis Law was no shrinking violet either, to say the least.

Certainly, the City lads were not alone in their aggression. Around this time a fierce rivalry was developing between City and Leeds United, and any time we met we would be kicking lumps out of each other. But strange as it may seem, there was also great respect on both sides, and I think it is still there. City's captain Tony Book, at right-back, could dish it out when he wanted to, in a nice quiet way. Book was signed by Allison at the age of thirty-one from Plymouth Argyle, his former employer for whom he had earlier signed Book from non-league football. But Book's age was no disadvantage, except in the minds of other people, who tend to define any player over thirty entirely in age terms. In fact, I found Tony to be a top-class player, and deceptively quick. I think he could have played for England at the time, just after the World Cup win, when that would have been a very hard thing to achieve.

Colin Bell did play for England many times and captained them once. He was really a right-sided midfield player, and Malcolm could not speak highly enough of him, calling him the best midfield player in Europe. He also gave him the nickname 'Nijinsky', probably after the famous racehorse of the time trained by Vincent O'Brien, rather than the Russian ballet dancer. It was a reference to Bell's athleticism and his tremendous attitude.

And there was Franny Lee, who had been a good player at his first club Bolton but who was regarded as a bit of a rebel. City signed him anyway for £60,000 and he immediately set about making a major contribution to their drive for the league championship in 1967–1968. He scored in the last match at Newcastle, which City needed to win, and which they ended up winning well, 4–3. Franny had played a lot on the right wing at Bolton, but he was not scared of getting into any position. Again, he was a top-class player and very aggressive, with a great shot in his right foot. Franny, without doubt, was cocky. But that was no harm either, in a team full of personality in the best sense of the word. Malcolm, of course, was full of personality in a way that was bound to get him into trouble eventually, but the team he created won four trophies in three years – the league in 1967–1968, the FA Cup in 1969, and the League Cup and the European Cup Winners' Cup in 1970. They had come from nothing to reach these heights, playing in a very attractive and effective style.

With more success, Malcolm became less grounded. I think he resented Joe Mercer getting as much of the credit as he did, without realising how important Joe had been to him, how Joe allowed him to get on with what he was really good at, which was working with the players.

I'm told he actually used to drink with the lads, and perhaps it was in that frame of mind that the signing of Rodney Marsh in 1972 seemed like a good idea. City were leading the First Division at the time by four points, and with Joe now out of the picture, maybe it went to Malcolm's head a bit. Marsh was signed for £200,000, supposedly as the icing on the cake. Unfortunately that particular cake collapsed, and City ended up in fourth that season.

Not that the idea of the icing on the cake is always a bad one. But it can get a bit complicated.

At Tottenham you could say that Jimmy Greaves was the icing on the cake, but Dave Mackay was the cake. At Leeds in my time, Allan Clarke was the icing on the cake when he arrived from Leicester City. At Liverpool, you couldn't really say that vital signings such as Kevin Keegan or Kenny Dalglish were the icing on the cake – they were probably a bit of both. But when Alex Ferguson signed Eric Cantona, he was all icing, Roy Keane was the cake. And Keane would have been the cake in any other team, but Cantona would not necessarily have been the icing in another team. George Best was probably the icing – but very good icing – on a cake made by Bobby Charlton and Nobby Stiles. At Arsenal, Dennis Bergkamp was the icing on a Bruce Rioch cake – but it was a pretty dull cake. Some say that Marco van Basten, Ruud Gullit and Frank Rijkaard were the icing on the cake made by Paolo Maldini and Franco Baresi for AC Milan, though in fact they all helped to make that particular cake.

Real players, on the whole, tend to be part icing, part cake. And yet players who are all icing, like Cantona, can be just what a team needs and they can play a huge part in a team's success – especially if they are finishers. Sadly the icing that was Rodney Marsh on the cake that was Manchester City was never going to be a success.

But the run they had was remarkable at a time when the competition was so intense. It wasn't just Manchester United and Liverpool now, there was a very good Chelsea team that had been developed out of a youth policy pursued under Tommy Docherty. This had produced players such as Bobby Tambling, John Hollins, Terry Venables, Peter Osgood, Barry Bridges and Ron Harris, and they were joined by signings such as Eddie McCreadie, Charlie Cooke, Ian Hutchinson and Peter Houseman. In fact, success was becoming so difficult to achieve that that Chelsea team, for all its talented players, never mounted a serious challenge for the league. After City had won it, a different team won the league in each of the next five seasons, starting with Leeds United, then Everton, Arsenal, Derby County and a re-emerging Liverpool.

Chelsea managed to win the FA Cup in 1970 and the Cup Winners' Cup in 1971, but theirs was mainly a story of what could-have-been and what should-have-been. From that youth team, Bobby Tambling emerged as a good striker, very game. Terry Venables had been a wonder boy, and he became a good player, a very thoughtful player, but he had no pace. As the Chelsea team evolved, that stopped him becoming the top-class player he had promised to be.

Peter Osgood was one of the most talented players I've come

across, and he should have been a great player. He was a big lad, with good control, an intelligent player. But I think they had a high-living style at Chelsea, which would have been no great help to players like him, Alan Hudson or Charlie Cooke. Hudson was another player of immense ability who promised great things. Charlie Cooke was an absolutely brilliant dribbler, who could cause a lot of problems for the opposition, but his career was over too quickly.

There were individuals coming along at other clubs around that time who also fitted into that could-have-been category. Tony Currie at Sheffield United had tremendous talent, and I think he had the ability to become one of the great midfield players. His passing was good, and he had vision and excellent technique all round. Through a combination of injuries, and maybe not looking after himself as well as he could have done, Tony didn't realise his potential.

Players such as Frank Worthington, Rodney Marsh and Duncan McKenzie were in a slightly different bracket – they were entertainers. They would do tricks, their technique was good in a circus-type of way that the crowd enjoyed. I've met Worthington, and I liked him. Duncan too was a good lad, who played for Leeds towards the end of my time there. Marsh was another who entertained the crowd, but I couldn't see any of them in a championship-winning team. I couldn't see them playing for Liverpool when Liverpool were expected to win things, year in and year out. I wouldn't quite call them could-have-beens, because they didn't have the real talent of the could-have-beens, the Osgoods, the Hudsons, the Cookes, the Curries – those players could have done it, the entertainers were never going to do it. But they won the affection of a lot of people, and good luck to them for that.

Probably in a category all on his own, we find Derek Dougan. He led a good Wolves team in the 1970s, with players such as Kenny Hibbitt, Mike Bailey, David Wagstaffe, Derek Parkin and John Richards, managed by Bill McGarry. But Dougan was very underrated. He suffered from being known as a 'character' from his early days at Blackburn Rovers where, among other things, he had asked for a transfer on the morning of the 1960 FA Cup final – a match in which Blackburn were playing. Back then they used to call him 'Cheyenne', on account of his most distinctive haircut which was not unlike the mohican style that came later. 'The Doog' was highly intelligent, but it seemed that he went out of his way to be controversial. From Blackburn, he went to Aston Villa and down all the way to Peterborough United in the Third Division, at which point it looked like he was out of it. But at Peterborough, like St Paul, Derek Dougan underwent some sort of a conversion. He was transferred to Leicester City, where he did quite well, playing as he could play, and then at Wolves he had the best part of his career. Without doubt, Dougan was one of the best strikers in the country. He was a big lad, strong, exceptionally quick, a good finisher. At last, Derek Dougan became the player he should have been.

Tony Brown at West Bromwich Albion was another terrific goal scorer of that time – in all he scored about 280 goals from midfield for West Brom. With his great attitude on and off the pitch, there was no could-have-been or should-have-been with Tony. He really was a wonderful player.

Chelsea could have done with him, but they were not alone

in their underachievement. There was a very good Tottenham team that won the League Cup in 1971 and 1973 and the UEFA Cup in 1972, but which could not win either of the big two domestic trophies. The Spurs Double-winning team had broken up quickly, and for most of the 1960s they were rebuilding, but by the end of the decade it was an impressive-looking side, with players such as Pat Jennings, Joe Kinnear, Cyril Knowles, Mike England, Alan Mullery, Alan Gilzean and Steve Perryman.

In Jennings, Spurs had one of the great players. Pat hadn't started off very well, probably a bit nervous, to the extent that the old keeper Bill Brown was brought back in to replace the man who was supposed to be replacing him. But when Jennings got going, it was clear that he had the perfect temperament to be a goalkeeper. He never seemed to get excited about anything that was happening on the pitch. He was a good athlete and he had great hands, which he partly attributed to the fact that he had played a lot of Gaelic football in his youth – he would catch the ball with one hand, just like a Gaelic footballer fielding a high ball.

A consistent level of excellence is the hallmark of the top-class keeper, though special mention should be made of a particular day at Anfield when Jennings saved two penalties, the first from Kevin Keegan, the second from Tommy Smith. Apparently Keegan and Smith had argued over who was going to take the first one, so there was no doubt about who was going to take the second. It made no difference, Pat saved them both.

Pat Jennings was outstanding even by comparison with all the excellent English keepers of that time. Which brings us to another development in the game, one that we could have done without, and one that is almost as mysterious as the disappearance of the great Scottish footballer – or even the good Scottish footballer. I refer to the virtual disappearance of the great British goalkeeper – or even the good British goalkeeper.

When I was playing, apart from Jennings, there was still Gordon Banks, Peter Shilton, Ray Clemence, Phil Parkes, Peter Bonetti, Gordon West and Alex Stepney. Today, the breed is virtually extinct, with Joe Hart the only top-class English goalkeeper in the entire Premier League, and Shay Given holding the fort for Ireland. The rest are all from Spain and the Czech Republic and Poland and even the United States.

Peter Schmeichel from Denmark became perhaps the best goalkeeper ever to play in England, a huge presence and a major influence for Manchester United when they began to win trophies in the 1990s. I would put Petr Čech of Chelsea up with the best of them before his head injury in 2006 – I don't think he's been quite the same since, but he is still one of the best kickers of a ball I have ever seen, and that includes outfield players. Pepe Reina at Liverpool is also outstanding. And yet, not only were foreign keepers almost unheard of in the old First Division, in my day we regarded them as a joke. Any time we were playing in Europe, we always felt we had a chance mainly because of the keepers. We would always be putting pressure on them from corner kicks and free kicks, because we knew they didn't like it. Admittedly you were allowed to be more physical at the time in challenging the keeper. But they were generally a poor lot.

So this Spurs side which was only a 'cup team' at the time – and the minor cups at that – had one of the great goalkeepers, and in front of him in defence he had players like Cyril Knowles and Joe Kinnear, both good footballers, and Mike England, an outstanding cente-half. England, who was also the captain of Wales, was a good header of the ball and had reasonably good control. In midfield, there was Alan Mullery, a solid player, and Steve Perryman, always a good-hearted lad, who later captained the team from full-back. In that position, I thought he was good enough to play for England. Jimmy Greaves, of course, was still there, still scoring goals and forming an excellent partnership with Alan Gilzean, a really intelligent player. Gilzean had an excellent positional sense, which meant that he never looked like he was running around. He was a great glancer of a ball, who knew exactly where he was heading it. Gilzean, a Scot, was as relaxed in his own way as Greaves himself. Ralph Coates, by contrast, was a busy type of player. And there was Martin Peters, another interesting figure in the evolution of the game.

When Alf Ramsey said that Martin Peters was ten years ahead of his time, a lot of people found it amusing, but of course Ramsey was right. Martin Peters was nominally regarded as a midfield player, but I never regarded him as such – I considered him a striker. He had a very good instinct for getting into the box from deep positions. Personally, if I was playing midfield, I wouldn't often be getting into the box, because I'd be backing the game up, whereas Martin would be going into the box all the time.

Peters was called 'The Ghost' because of this ability he had to suddenly appear in a very dangerous position, and perhaps also because he could go ten minutes without touching the ball

– again this is why I didn't regard him as a midfield player, and why I used to resent him a bit, given that I was a midfield player myself in the traditional sense. You mightn't see Martin in the game for long periods, but because of his other attributes, you had to live with it. Certainly in the right team, he was a big asset. He was very good for England, as long as they had Alan Ball, Bobby Charlton and Nobby Stiles doing what was needed in the middle. Meanwhile Martin could be operating as this striker playing from deep, and because of his mobility, it was very hard to pick him up until it was too late. He was also a good finisher and a very good header of the ball. And sure enough, as Ramsey had predicted, eventually we started to see players like David Platt doing what Martin Peters had done. You can even see a bit of Peters in players like Steven Gerrard and Frank Lampard, who are considered to be midfield players but who don't really play that role in the true sense, and are probably most valuable to their teams as finishers.

Good as they were, that Spurs team, like Chelsea, were not really going neck and neck with Manchester City to claim that ultimate prize of the league. They may have had a bit of that laid-back London thing about them, maybe the competition was just too intense at the time. The next season, it was Leeds United who took over from City at the top. We had been building up to it for a few years, reaching the FA Cup final in 1965, finishing second in the league in 1965–1966, winning the League Cup and the Fairs Cup in 1967–1968, before finally winning the league itself in 1968–1969.

Leeds also changed the game, in terms of Don Revie's emphasis on professionalism, but it wouldn't have been seen as a force for good at the time. There was a lot of criticism of Big Jack Charlton 'going under the bar' at corner kicks, or of a Leeds player taking the ball to the corner flag near the end of a game to run down the clock. Leeds were accused of the most cynical gamesmanship, doing things that are now regarded as perfectly normal – indeed you can often hear players being lambasted by commentators when their team is leading and they have the ball near the corner flag in injury time, and they try something fancy instead of holding it there.

But over the years, there has also been a real appreciation of the quality of that Leeds team, and I think it is best demonstrated by the fact that so many people can name the Leeds first eleven of that era, without thinking too hard about it. In fact, I'm not sure if the same can be said of any other English team in modern history, except maybe the England team that won the World Cup and perhaps one of the great Liverpool teams. Even the great Manchester United team of Charlton, Best and Law had a lot of other fine players in it, but it would be a challenge to anyone who is not a United fan to name the whole team as easily as they would reel off the names of Terry Cooper, Paul Madeley, Paul Reaney, Norman Hunter, Billy Bremner, Peter Lorimer, Mick Jones, Allan Clarke, Eddie Gray and so on. Probably many people could name Nobby Stiles and Alex Stepney along with the big stars from that United team. Likewise everyone remembers Summerbee, Bell and Lee at City, but you don't hear as much about the others, the Glyn Pardoes and the Neil Youngs. And in the case of the West Ham team containing the England trio of Bobby Moore, Martin Peters and Geoff Hurst, I would say that even West Ham fans might be hard pressed to name the rest of that team.

So apart from all the controversy, there is obviously something about Leeds United under Don Revie that has stayed with people, for the right reasons. And partly, I think, it is because we were around at the top for so long. We were neck and neck with City for a while, but when they faded away, we stayed up there. City won their four trophies in three seasons, whereas we got to our first major final in 1965, and we were still able to win the league with substantially the same squad in 1974, reaching the European Cup final in 1975. That was a very, very long time to be competing at the highest level, at home and in Europe.

Arsenal did it all in the one season, winning the Double in 1971–1972 with really good players such as Frank McLintock, Peter Storey, Pat Rice, George Armstrong, George Graham and Bob McNab, a fabulous achievement without a doubt. And Everton with Alan Ball, Howard Kendall and Colin Harvey in midfield – again we remember three of them – had their one big year in 1970 before going into decline, with Ball leaving for Arsenal. At Derby County a thirty-seven-year-old manager called Brian Clough was about to reveal his genius to the world, winning the league in 1972 with players like Alan Hinton, Roy McFarland, John O'Hare and Alan Durban – in passing it should be noted that Derby had been promoted in 1968 with the help of a certain Dave Mackay. But I don't think it is being boastful to say that Leeds outlasted the lot of them, by some distance – it is just the plain fact of the matter.

And the other reason that people remember that team so

Stanley Matthews, the original 'wizard of dribble' and one of my earliest inspirations.

Tom Finney. Whatever the weather, either on the wing or centre-forward – great.

Danny Blanchflower, rebellious spirit, great mind, top player.

Spurs legend Dave Mackay.

Goal-scoring genius Jimmy Greaves (watched by teammate Terry Venables).

George Best (Mike England behind). One of the most gifted, whose star faded prematurely.

Bobby Charlton. The best.

Denis Law, a force of nature on the pitch.

Ian St John: 'The Saint', and at times he played like one.

Nobby Stiles (tackling Jimmy Greaves). Application, attitude, ability, World Cup winner.

Francis Lee, a major player in a terrific City team.

Mike Summerbee,
excellent player and
anything but a
soft-touch winger.

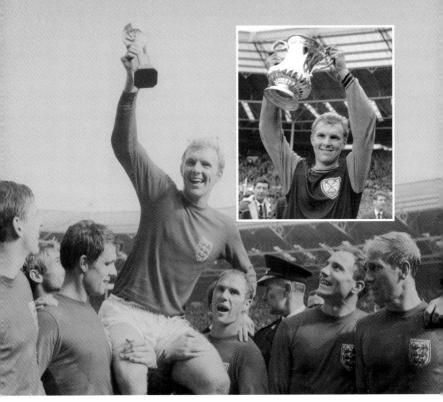

Bobby Moore: The greater the challenge, the better he was.

Jimmy Johnstone. At his best, unstoppable.

Norman Hunter: 'bites your legs' but could really play.

John Robertson, underrated genius.

well is the simplest and the best reason – the players. There wasn't a Best or a Charlton at Leeds, the ability was more evenly spread. Don had taken these young lads – who were not the Busby Babes, not the most prodigious talents – and he had turned them into players who could stand up in their own right as being world class. At one point, there were sixteen internationals in the squad, and most of them could easily make their way into any fair-minded Hall of Fame.

At the end of the 1960s and the start of the 1970s, both Leeds United and Manchester City did it in their own way, and they did it with players of great ability and attitude. And people don't forget that.

6

Rich Man,
Poor Man, Wild Man

In 1967, Mike Summerbee and George Best went into business together, running a boutique in Manchester. Mike was not quite as extravagant as Malcolm Allison, but he was a flamboyant guy in his own right, who wasn't shy of publicity – George got publicity without trying.

People tend to laugh these days when they think of that time when footballers were running boutiques, but it probably wasn't quite as mad as it sounds. All of us had to work out some way to make a living after we quit football, for the simple reason that there was never the slightest chance of us accumulating enough money during our playing careers to last us the rest of our lives. These days an average player in a mid-table Premier League team can be almost set up for life after a few seasons, but back in the days when Mike Summerbee and George Best were running a boutique, it was a bit more complicated.

Mike, in that championship-winning year of 1968, probably wasn't making much more than £50 a week at City. I was doing a bit better at Leeds United, but not much, on £60 a week. This was about twice as much as what I'd been getting at Manchester United towards the end of my time there, but you still couldn't retire on it. So it was always in the back of your mind that you might need to turn your hand to something other than football eventually. And if you were as well known and popular and fashion-conscious as those two lads were, it must have seemed pretty smart to open such a shop – as I recall, it was a boutique for men. I don't know if Mike and George made any money on their joint-venture, but I suspect they did not. No more than the rest of us, they were not qualified to run a business.

Which didn't stop us trying, and failing. Jimmy Greaves had a sports shop for a while. A lot of lads tried to run pubs, which again might have seemed like a good idea at first but which was probably not a good idea at all on a number of levels. Some of us, if we were lucky, went on to make a living at something related to the game itself – you could say we were qualified at that. Ideally there would be some sort of work in the media, and some players did quite well on the after-dinner circuit. These days, many can be found in hospitality suites on match days, a role which is pleasant enough, if they can ignore the fact that there are fellows out on the pitch getting paid more in a week that they got in a year – without having nearly as much talent.

Not that I have any problem with the money that footballers make these days, by comparison to the money in my day. The point I am making here is how different *that* world was to the football world that we know today, and how ridiculous some of the structures of the game still were. While my contemporaries in the 1960s and 1970s seemed for all the world like the most modern young men, with quite glamorous lives, driving sports cars and even modelling, in the overall sweep of history they were probably victims to the same extent that Wilf Mannion was. They might have enjoyed the fame and the fact that they were getting paid a bit more than the average man, but the fortunes were still being made by other people.

In fact, I can think of just two players who made fortunes entirely created by themselves at something other than football. One was Dave Whelan, well known these days as the owner of Wigan, who played for Blackburn Rovers and who broke his leg in the 1960 cup final against Wolves. Later he played for Crewe Alexandra, before starting a chain of supermarkets which made him his first million. The other person was Mike Summerbee's partner in football, Francis Lee. I believe that Franny had started looking for alternative sources of income way back when he was at Bolton, so clearly there was always a business brain at work there. And as for his competitive edge, no one would be in any doubt about that if they witnessed the famous fist-fight that broke out at the Baseball Ground in 1975 between Franny – who had moved to Derby County with whom he would win another league medal – and Norman Hunter. They were even sent off for it, a rare enough sanction at the time, and with Lee's nose bloodied, they continued to fight on the way to the dressing room, the sort of scene that in today's game would have them talking about twelve-match bans.

There had been a penalty in the match that Lee had scored after he himself was supposedly fouled. But Norman saw it as a dive. Terrific player though he was, Lee had a reputation as a diver. And Norman was taunting him about this during the match – 'You little shit, fucking diving, you're always fucking diving,' he said. Or words to that effect. Norman also got his punch in first, and Franny would have been boiling about this. So when they were both sent off, and they were walking off the pitch, I believe there were some verbals, with Norman probably adding to his earlier criticisms. Franny was very aggressive, and having already received that punch in the nose, something that he would not have taken lightly, he lashed out.

A successful career in business seemed unlikely at that moment, but then Franny turned out to be an exception. Not only did he become very successful in the paper industry – toilet paper mainly – he even became a horse trainer for a while. He should be viewed as a sort of a wonder of the footballing world, totally unlike so many of his contemporaries. When he won that second title at Derby, his manager was Dave Mackay, who appreciated the nature of Franny's other commitments by allowing him to continue living in Manchester. But Dave's old manager at Tottenham, Bill Nicholson, the man who won the Double, had just a minor role at the club at this stage and was still living in quite a small house near White Hart Lane. It was the same house he had lived in when he was a Spurs player, a time when most players lived within walking distance of the grounds, because they couldn't afford a car.

It seems scandalous now, when Fabio Capello could be paid about £6 million a year for managing England with limited success, that a man such as Nicholson who achieved something thought to be virtually impossible was living in such a humble way. But he was most certainly not the only one.

In earlier chapters, we have described the huge influence that a few great managers had on the development of the game, the glorious victories that they enjoyed. But at the height of his success at Leeds, for example, Don Revie was never on more than £15,000 a year. While Matt Busby was creating an empire at United, others were making the fortunes. And Shankly's life after leaving Liverpool was famously miserable, partly because he just couldn't stay away from the club he loved. As we know, in any walk of life, if a retired man just keeps going back to his place of work, it can make life difficult for all concerned. Eventually he stayed away, becoming estranged enough from Liverpool to start appearing at the Everton training ground which was near his house. And he said with great sadness that he was more warmly received there than he was at Liverpool. His house, like that of Bill Nicholson – and unlike that of, say, Sven-Goran Eriksson – was semi-detached.

And yet, while the great managers were victims of the

prevailing culture of the time as much as the players, that very way of doing things was also vital to their success. I had dealings with three of them – Matt Busby, Don Revie and Brian Clough – and all of them may well have been successful in today's environment but, for that to happen, they would have had to do things very differently. Clough at Derby County and later at Nottingham Forest built championship-winning teams with his astute signings of good players, but these days he could be outdone by a much lesser manager who just has more money to spend. Hundreds of millions more. As for Busby and Revie, they benefited greatly from the system whereby there was no freedom of contract for the players as there is today. Both of them would have found it very hard to build a team now, when players can negotiate or leave when their contracts expire.

There would probably have been no Busby Babes in today's environment, because the team would not have stayed together as long as they did. Today, those brilliant young players would be attracted away by the offer of much better wages. But in the 1950s, you couldn't move anyway – when you signed for a club at seventeen, you signed for life. Any move you made after that was at the club's discretion. So with that mindset among the players, and no danger of it changing for the forseeable future, Busby could keep that team together for long enough to realise their potential together at United.

Don Revie, under today's conditions, would also have been in a predicament. If a player like Norman Hunter had an agent, after three seasons during which Norman had shown how good he was, the agent could have gone to Don Revie and demanded a move to another club – otherwise he would just let the contract run down, and Leeds would receive nothing. But, of course, Norman didn't have an agent, because there wasn't much point in having one. You were tied to whatever contract you had signed, for the full term, and then the club could decide if they wanted to sell you. They had all the power.

If the players had the power, as they do today, Don Revie would have found it almost impossible to bring on all those young lads as he did. Because the moment that Billy Bremner or Eddie Gray or Peter Lorimer started showing signs of real promise, most likely they would have been bought by the highest bidder and paid a lot more than Leeds in the Second Division could pay them.

As for myself, when Leeds won the league in 1969, I had been there for six years. I had established my reputation and the team had just become champions. If I'd had freedom of contract, I might well have been receiving a big-money offer from some other club, even from a club in Spain or Italy. And I think I would have taken it. Even though I was happy at Leeds, I would have taken it. But unlike the players of today, I did not have those temptations. We can see how players such as Wayne Rooney or Fernando Torres have the mindset that there is effectively no contract with the club, so if they want to go, they will go – whether the manager likes it or not.

Perhaps the strangest case of all was that of Carlos Tevez, who made an unbelievable stand against Roberto Mancini at Manchester City, unbelievable at least for those of us who grew up in football when Duncan Edwards was getting less than twenty quid a week. What is most unusual about the Tevez situation is that his attitude on the pitch is always brilliant, regardless of any hostilities that are taking place elsewhere. When Tevez goes out to play, he really plays. And because he is a terrific player, he tends to make a difference. I have often seen lads who are in dispute with their club who will just stop contributing in any sense. Tevez, in his own baffling way, will come back after a few months on the golf course and make a genuine effort to help you win the league.

You could summarise it like this – when I was playing, it was a better time for the game all round, but comparatively dreadful for the players; today it is a brilliant time for the players, but to the detriment of the game. No one seems to be able to find some happy medium, it is one extreme or the other. And one of the unfortunate side-effects of this is that players who are not performing as they should are protected in ways that they weren't under the old regime. Nobody minds the top players getting as much money as they can, and good luck to them, but you also have the likes of Joey Barton becoming extraordinarily rich. And Stephen Ireland hardly kicked a ball in three years, a mystery throughout his career to various managers who probably thought they had the magic formula that could get the best out of him.

In any case, finances are usually more important than good management these days. Who knows what David Moyes at Everton could achieve if all the other Premier League managers had as little money as he does? Could he have been like Clough, with his eye for a player or at least Peter Taylor's eye for a player, winning the league with the brilliance of his signings? Certainly I don't think that Roberto Mancini would have won the Premier League if City had been working on a budget roughly similar to Everton's. I don't think anyone could have done that.

Money has distorted everything, so that an Arab billionaire can simply choose a club on which to bestow endless riches, and no matter what a good manager like Moyes does, he can never hope to win. You build a football empire these days with money, not with the genius of one man.

And there were no foreign players in my time either, there was much less movement in the market all round. Probably the most extreme example of the nurturing of local talent was the Celtic team managed by the great Jock Stein that won the European Cup in 1967 – the team consisted of players who were all born within a thirty-mile radius of Parkhead. Today, people marvel at players like Steven Gerrard and Jamie Carragher, local lads still playing for the club that they grew up with, so the notion of all eleven players being local lads seems very far-fetched. But that is what they were, Ronnie Simpson, Jim Craig, Tommy Gemmell, Bobby Murdoch, Billy McNeill, John Clark, Jimmy Johnstone, Willie Wallace, Stevie Chalmers, Bertie Auld and Bobby Lennox – a bit like that Leeds team, the names seem to stay with you. But if Leeds were a phenomenon that lasted from the mid-1960s well into the 1970s, a kind of team that hadn't been there before, then Celtic were a greater phenomenon. They had the same sort of professionalism that we had at Leeds, but Jock Stein was able to strike a happy balance between that professionalism and a sense of freedom.

Again, because of the system that prevailed at the time,

Jock was able to build his team. Bertie Auld had gone from Celtic to Birmingham, where he was a good left-winger in a mediocre team, but he returned to Celtic to play in midfield. He was a truly great player. Bobby Murdoch was outstanding, Jimmy Johnstone was an astonishing player. Absolutely brilliant.

Jimmy was a strange lad, who was once supposed to play for Scotland against England at Wembley but got off the train at Carlisle. He didn't fancy it. The idea of going any farther into England seemed to trouble him greatly. On another notorious occasion in the build-up to a game against England at Hampden in the 1974 Home Internationals, the Scotland players were watching England playing Northern Ireland at Wembley on the television in their training camp at Largs. It was a game that England won 1–0, which meant that the match at Hampden would be the decider – but there was more than the Home Internationals exciting the minds of the Scottish players. They were also on their way to the 1974 World Cup, the only one of the four 'Home' countries to qualify. Taking all these things into account, they felt that they were obliged to have a 'drinks party'. And as drinks parties with Scotland players tend to do, it got out of hand.

After a long night of carousing in Largs, it was getting light when they were walking up the beach, and a few of them, including Jimmy Johnstone, spotted a rowing boat. As Jimmy got into the boat, the other lads pushed the boat out, and with a growing sense of drunken horror they began to realise that Jimmy was adrift – there were no rowlocks to take the oars. And so the great Jimmy Johnstone was drifting out to sea, to be eventually rescued by the coastguard service. It became a national scandal to everyone except Jimmy Johnstone, who particularly resented the reaction of the manager Willie Ormond. In a team meeting to discuss the incident, Johnstone apparently said to Ormond, 'You're giving me some fucking look, sir', as if Ormond had no right to be so critical. Unsurprisingly, Scotland went on to beat England 2–0 at Hampden, with Johnstone the star. There is a photograph out there of Johnstone bare-chested after the match, giving the 'up yours' V-sign, supposedly to the press. Or is it to Willie Ormond, who can also be seen in the picture with his back turned to Johnstone? It is hard to tell.

I think the Celtic players used to protect Jimmy from himself, but unfortunately in the European Cup semi-final of 1970, Leeds had no protection from the genius of Jimmy Johnstone. He tore us apart. He was smaller than me, but he could beat any player with his dribbling. They talk about players changing a game, but Jimmy really could do that. The ball would come to him after the good play of the others, but it certainly encourages that good play if you have someone there like Jimmy Johnstone who can do the sort of damage that he did.

England had won the World Cup in 1966 on their own ground, but Celtic won the European Cup in 1967 in Lisbon against Inter Milan, a team which had already won the European Cup in 1964 and 1965 and were strong favourites to win it for the third time in four years. Inter had top-class players such as Sandro Mazzola and Giacinto Facchetti and Renato Cappellini, and a legendary manager in Helenio Herrera who had them playing the famous 'catenaccio' system. It was an extemely defensive system that Inter Milan played so well it almost guaranteed that if they scored one goal, the game would be over. That was what usually happened anyway, until they came up against Jock Stein's Celtic, who went out there and blew them off the park.

I saw that match again recently on television, and it confirmed everything I felt about it at the time. Celtic were brilliant, playing with that professionalism but also that freedom instilled in them by Stein, taking on these guys and beating them well. Even when they went behind to an early goal, a penalty scored by Mazzola, their attitude to the game didn't change. And when Tommy Gemmell got the equaliser early in the second half, the pattern stayed the same, with Celtic playing all the football and Inter Milan thinking they could just keep them out with their 'catenaccio'. Milan might have had that reputation for rarely losing a lead, but Celtic believed in themselves enough to stay positive and keep taking them on. It wasn't just a matter of having the right attitude either, they had the players to do it too. When a shot from Bobby Murdoch was turned in by Stevie Chalmers five minutes from the end, Celtic had got their reward.

British teams in general did well in Europe in the 1960s, with West Ham and Tottenham winning the Cup Winners' Cup and Leeds United and Newcastle winning the Fairs Cup, but it was Celtic who made the biggest breakthrough. There is probably another book to be written about how eleven players born and raised in Scotland could destroy a team of top-class and highly paid Italians in such a devastating style on such a big occasion. And how such a thing would be totally inconceiveable today. Don't forget, in my time and for some time after that, almost all the successful teams in England had a Scottish or an Irish element, or ideally both. These days, even the top teams in Scotland don't have much of a Scottish element. It's as if a whole species has disappeared off the face of the earth, for all sorts of reasons, which are no doubt only partly to do with football.

These great football men like Bill Shankly, Matt Busby and Jock Stein all came from very tough mining backgrounds, which no doubt formed their character and made them feel privileged to be able to make a living at something as exciting and as glamorous as football. All of us back then, almost without exception, came from poor backgrounds in England, Ireland, Scotland or Wales, but the Scots seemed to have that slightly harder edge – or maybe the accent just made it sound that way. Maybe the fact that we still have a lot of Scottish managers out there suggests that the Scottish voice is still powerful in the game on the touchline. But not on the pitch.

One of the most celebrated Scottish victories was the 3–2 defeat of England at Wembley in 1967, the season after England had become world champions, a result that made the Scots feel as if they were now unoffically the best team in the world. No doubt it will always be a glorious memory, and yet as they recall the names of the players who beat England on that day, the Scots must weep for how it has all gone wrong. The Scotland team was: Simpson (Celtic), Gemmell (Celtic), McCreadie (Chelsea), Greig (Rangers), McKinnon (Rangers), Baxter (Sunderland), Wallace (Celtic), Bremner (Leeds),

McCalliog (Sheffield Wednesday), Law (Manchester United) and Lennox (Celtic). There was a time when you could easily have picked three good teams for Scotland, now you could hardly pick three good players.

And yet always with Scotland, even at the peak of their powers, there was this element of self-destruction. That famous win at Wembley is largely remembered in folklore for the performance of Jim Baxter, who slowed the game down at one point with a spot of 'keepy-uppy', teasing and taunting the English. There is no doubt that Jim Baxter was an absolutely brilliant player, and equally no doubt that he was a complete headbanger. In that, he was fairly typical of some of the more gifted Scottish players down the years – and one or two who were not so gifted. Clearly Jim had been brilliant from an early age, because Don Revie had heard about him when he was a teenager at Raith Rovers and had been interested in signing him for Leeds. Don was very meticulous in all things, but especially about the character of the player. So he put together a list of all the misbehaviour on Jim's part that had been described to him, and he went up to Jim's house in Fife to discuss it with the young man himself – drinking, of course, was the main one, along with not training properly and generally messing about. 'What do you think of this?' Don said to Jim, referring to the list. Jim considered what Don was putting to him, and he said, 'That's a big list, Don … a very big list … but there's a few fucking things even you haven't got in there.'

'Thanks very much, Jim,' Don replied, concluding the meeting.

So Baxter signed for Rangers, where he shone brightly

and brilliantly for a relatively short time in terms of his overall career. He had beautiful control, and was left-footed, somewhat in the style of Liam Brady. He could really play, and he was part of a Rangers team that dominated Celtic in the early 1960s, with excellent players like John Greig, Willie Henderson, Ralph Brand, Eric Caldow and Bobby Shearer. But Baxter appeared not to have much interest in training. Still, he was getting away with it until the night that he broke his leg in a European match in 1964. The story goes that the Rangers lads went to visit him in hospital, to find Jim already with a bottle of Bacardi on the table beside the bed.

Ideally if you get a serious injury, you recuperate in such a way that you come back in better overall condition than you were before. You work on other parts of your fitness, so that when the injury heals, you are stronger all round. That was not Jim's way, and so he moved on to Sunderland, where his talent could still be seen in flashes, but where his large belly could also now be seen – the nickname 'Slim Jim' was heavily ironic. Jim didn't give a damn. He moved on to Nottingham Forest, where he played alongside Terry Hennessey and Billy McKinlay – by a happy coincidence Hennessy is a well-known brandy, and Mackinlay is a brand of Scotch whisky. I recall that the Leeds trainer Syd Owen, who did not usually have much of a sense of humour, told us that the Forest half-back line on the day would be Hennessey, McKinlay and Bacardi.

By the time Bacardi Jim returned to Rangers, you might have expected him to buckle down a bit, as other lads might have done if they were given a last chance. But it was not to be. On international duty for Scotland, you'd hear stories of Jim climbing in the window in the training camp at Largs at two in the morning in time-honoured fashion. He was probably the ultimate example of those Scottish players who were natural footballers, but wild lads. They just had that trait, which was very attractive to the crowd in one way, but very dangerous in a lot of other ways. Certainly the Scottish crowd would have loved the way that Jim juggled the ball that day at Wembley, taking the piss out of the English lads. And the mind boggles at the amount of Bacardi he must have downed that night.

Then again, I spoke to Bobby Collins about him when we were at Leeds together, and Bobby wasn't so sure. 'Jim wouldn't be a patch on Billy Steel,' he said. Steel, a brilliant Scottish player of the post-war years, who was twice transferred for record fees, apparently made Jim Baxter look like a model professional. But they're all gone now, those wild Scottish lads, the good ones and especially the great ones.

Within a couple of generations, it seems that the football genius of that country has been passed on entirely to the managers, with Alex Ferguson in particular making sure that the Scottish influence is still strong. Though he would be the first to acknowledge that the tradition of the great Scottish manager may still be alive, it can never compensate for the loss of the great Scottish footballer – and the odd one who could be regarded as phenomenal. And in the face of the stiffest competition, the most phenomenal Scottish player of them all was probably Jimmy Johnstone, and the most phemonenal Scottish manager of them all was probably Jock Stein.

I think that I would just about place Stein ahead of even

Alex Ferguson for what he achieved as a manager. After he had won the European Cup, it is said that Stein had a conversation with Bill Shankly, in which Shankly told him, 'John, you are immortal now.' In that year, 1967, Celtic became the first team ever to win every competition they entered. Jock's record was sensational and, yet, like the other great managers of that era, he was a victim. I know that the Celtic players were paid a pittance and I have no doubt that Jock himself was as badly paid as the Inter Milan manager Helenio Herrera was highly paid – when Jock's team gave his team a right hiding in Lisbon, Herrera was reputed to be the best-paid manager in Europe.

Immortal though he was, when Jock was retiring as manager he was not offered a seat on the board at Celtic. Instead, the man who had won nine consecutive league titles was offered a job by the club in the Pools office. Again in these days of multimillion pay-offs to managers such as André Villas-Boas, the idea of this hugely successful football man being offered some small job in a fundraising capacity seems bizarre, bordering on the criminal. But that is how it was for Jock Stein, and for football men in general.

Jock used to like a gamble, which probably didn't help his finances either. I don't think he had any money when he left Celtic, and despite the millions he had made for the club, not to mention all the glory, they didn't look after him. But he didn't need money badly enough to take the job in the Pools office. As for what that offer did to his pride, we can only guess. He had been badly injured in a car accident in 1975, but he still felt that he had something to give to the game as a manager. As well he might. He came down to England to manage Leeds United for a few months in 1978, but he left soon afterwards when he was offered the job of Scotland manager.

In September 1985, Scotland drew 1–1 with Wales in Ninian Park in Cardiff, a result that would put them into the 1986 World Cup after a play-off against Australia. At the end of the match, Jock Stein had a heart attack and died soon afterwards in the stadium, at the age of sixty-two.

Among those who were most deeply affected by the passing of the great man was the one who would take his place as manager of Scotland at the World Cup – his assistant, the then manager of Aberdeen, Alex Ferguson.

7

A Bad Choice
and a Terrible Choice

The England team that went to the Mexico World Cup in 1970 was arguably better than the one that had won the competition in 1966. English football, and British football in general, still had this enormous prestige and was enjoying an extraordinary period of success. And yet in the years after 1966, you could hear quite a few voices saying that Alf Ramsey had ruined the game. They still lamented the fact that England were 'wingless wonders', which admittedly was one of the biggest changes in the game for a long, long time, but one that I believe Ramsey was entirely right to make.

As we have seen, it was not a plan that came from the skies, Ramsey was too wise for that. He did not have anything against wingers as such, he was pragmatic about these things – he was just responding to the fact that full-backs were now smaller and quicker. So he made a calculated decision that if he had two increasingly ineffective wingers playing, he could not have Alan Ball and Martin Peters in the team. And he needed Ball and Peters, with their energy and their class, more than he needed a Terry Paine or a Peter Thompson out there dribbling in an attractive style but with limited results. Indeed, Alan Ball was a really outstanding player, who was only twenty-one and still playing with Blackpool when England won the World Cup. He was a bright and breezy sort of a player, who could play in midfield and score goals as well, certainly in the early part of his career. Ball won the league with Everton in 1970, and I think that Everton as a club was always his big love. He joined Arsenal after they won the Double, but I don't think he really did it for them. There was no doubt, though, that he did it for England.

But always in football there is that copycat effect, and now a lot of teams had started to copy Ramsey by getting rid of the out-and-out winger. Indeed they copied it to such an extent that, to this day, you will not see many such wingers. You will see the four midfielders rather than the two midfielders and the two wingers. There is more emphasis now on midfielders multitasking, rather than the specialist roles of old. I suppose in the present day, Theo Walcott could be regarded as an out-and-out winger, up to a point. But then he is not much good. Ryan Giggs was an out-and-out winger for a while, but then he moved more towards a midfield role. And David Beckham was never a winger in the classic sense.

In Mexico, there was a player who would definitely have been picked by Ramsey for his 1970 team, and for his 1966 team too if he had been available, proving that Ramsey wasn't tied to some rigid belief in football without wingers, just for its own sake. Unfortunately the player in question wasn't available for England. In fact, in the first game in the group stage in Guadalajara he was playing against England for Brazil. His name was Jairzinho. At a time when many wingers were becoming obsolete, he could still do it, beating players as good as Terry Cooper at full-back. Jairzinho was strong, he could make goals and he could score goals – he scored the only goal of that game against England. Jairzinho was, in fact, one of the best players I have ever seen.

And his amazing performances on the wing were now being seen by a global TV audience in colour. We saw so little, only glimpses, of the Brazil stars of the 1958 World Cup, such as Garrincha or the young Pelé – they were a part of our imagination along with Matthews or Finney. Of course, television in general throughout the 1960s was starting to change the way that everyone related to the game. The British stations had started showing a lot more football than the days when highlights of the cup final were the only moving pictures available. And we were also being exposed more to continental and international football in general, all of which broadened the popularity of the game and its finances, and increased our knowledge. But there was something about the impact of the Mexico World Cup of 1970, and that Brazil team in particular, that took the game to a different level all round. Today, Jairzinho would be one of the wonders of the world, but in that Brazil team, of course, he was not the only one.

And that tournament is regarded with special affection by any football fan who happened to be around at that time, not just for the pleasure of watching that magnificent Brazilian team but because the time difference meant that viewers in this part of the world were watching some of the games late at night. People have told me it was like seeing something from another planet, such was the novelty of being able to watch so much of the tournament on TV at such strange kick-off times.

Oddly enough, I was not one of the lucky ones watching Pelé and Jairzinho and Gerson and Tostão and Carlos Alberto in that way, because I was actually in Mexico. This was quite a strange state of affairs in itself, the result of a competition in a TV magazine whereby a panel picked a Great Britain eleven for the World Cup, from goalkeeper to outside-left. And then the readers made their own selections. And if the choice of the reader coincided with that of the panel, the reader would get to go to Mexico with the eleven players that the expert panel had picked. It sounds a bit complicated but, at the end of it all, eleven players and eleven members of the general public went off to Mexico for what was basically an all-expenses-paid holiday. The players included myself and Billy Bremner, John Greig and Colin Stein of Rangers, Bobby Hope of West Brom and Terry Hennessey (who had just been transferred from Nottingham Forest to Derby County for £100,000) – all members of this mythical Great Britain team. We were based in Guadalajara, where England were playing their group matches against Romania, Czechoslovakia and Brazil. So we were at that famous game in which Gordon Banks made his incredible save from Pelé's header, when Bobby Moore made that tackle on Pelé which has been seen so many times and when Jairzinho ran towards the touchline after he scored the goal, leaping with joy and punching the air, as if he had scored the winner in the final itself.

It was touch and go in the match, and with the score at 1–0, Jeff Astle of West Brom, who had come on as a sub, had a great chance when he was through on his own, with only the keeper to beat. He missed it. England were obviously disappointed to lose on the day, but they qualified anyway from the group with 1–0 wins in the other matches, and it had been an honourable defeat against Brazil. It was the next game, against West Germany in the quarter-final in León, which saw the beginning of the end of the career of Alf Ramsey, one of the great football men. And not only did things go badly wrong for England in that game, it can be seen as a turning point in the whole story of the English game. It can even be said that from that moment until the present day, England in general has hardly had a happy day at a major football tournament.

And maybe the saddest thing of all for Ramsey is that he didn't really do much wrong. With England leading 2–0 against West Germany, thanks to a goal by Alan Mullery after half an hour and one by Martin Peters early in the second half, Ramsey decided to take off Bobby Charlton. It was a red-hot day, and kick-off had been at noon to facilitate TV viewers in Europe. So with about twenty minutes left, thinking that the game was won, Ramsey wanted to save Bobby for the next game. And it made sense. Bobby was thirty-two at the time. I think if I'd been in Ramsey's position, I would have made the same decision.

But it turned out to be fatal. A shot from Beckenbauer went under the body of Peter Bonetti and changed the game. The decision to take off Bobby was made just before the goal was scored but it went ahead anyway as the Germans trotted back to their half in the appalling heat, now with new hope. Even if Ramsey had had the chance to keep Bobby on with the score at 2–1, I think he would have stuck by his original decision to substitute him.

As for playing without Gordon Banks, he had no choice. Bonetti was playing because Banks had been taken ill with food poisoning, another unlucky break for Ramsey on the face of it, but then in many ways Bonetti was not a bad replacement. He was savaged at the time for his performance in León, accused of losing his nerve on the big occasion, but again if it was up to me, and Banks was out, I would have had no problem in selecting Bonetti for that match.

Of course, as it turned out, he would have let me down, as he let Ramsey down, but there is no way of knowing that your keeper is going to have a bad day. You can only rely on your judgement of the player in general, and personally I rated Bonetti highly. He was a very good keeper who had just won the FA Cup with Chelsea against Leeds, a huge occasion both at Wembley and in the replay at Old Trafford, in which he had shown no such signs of weakness – it was our keeper Gary Sprake who 'threw one in'.

These things happen in football. I was still a Ramsey fan, but unfortunately for him most of the guys in the media were not. The fact that England had been world champions going into the tournament, the fact that they were still regarded as one of the best teams in the world, just behind Brazil, was not properly appreciated at the time. Now that we can look back and see that that Brazil team was one of the all-time great sides, we can see how good England were, with the star men of 1966 now joined by players like Francis Lee, Colin Bell and Allan Clarke, with Brian Labone in for Big Jack, Terry Cooper in for Ray Wilson and Alan Mullery in for Nobby Stiles. And yet, even at these heights which now seem so impressive, the process had already begun that would eventually bring Ramsey down. Basically, most of the media guys just didn't like him. He was abrupt and impatient with them, and they took it personally.

His attitude to what we now call 'public relations' was so dismissive, it can now be seen as heroic. 'Welcome to Scotland, Sir Alf,' he was once hailed. To which Sir Alf was heard to mutter, 'You must be fucking joking.' Or better, he was co-commentator at a match at which the floodlights failed, and he was asked when he thought the lights might come back. 'I am not an electrician,' he explained.

In more recent times, the process of getting rid of the England manager starts the day he takes the job, but in Ramsey's time things went at a slightly slower pace. And after all, he had been successful, which slowed things down a bit further. With a sympathetic or even a reasonable press, he would have been forgiven the various misfortunes of León, but that was not the case. In my experience, if a manager has a great relationship with the media, he doesn't usually have a great relationship with the players. There is a basic conflict between the two, with the media trying to get as much as they can, and the manager ideally giving them as little as he can. The media will always want a manager to criticise the players. But if he does that, the players will regard it as a betrayal and, at some point, he will lose them.

I knew from Nobby Stiles how much the players respected and trusted Ramsey in this regard. In the group stage of the 1966 World Cup, Nobby committed a foul against the French midfielder Jacques Simon, which had the press screaming for his removal from the team. But Ramsey pulled him aside a couple of days before the next match against Argentina in the quarter-final, and told him he would be playing regardless of all the criticism. That's the sort of thing that creates a bond with a player, and not just with that particular player but with the team in general – Nobby would have told the others about the manager's display of loyalty and, as we know, when it really mattered, Nobby did not let Alf down.

But the pressure was building after Mexico, the media growing increasingly hostile to Ramsey in this new era in which television was throwing up all sorts of football characters who seemed far more entertaining than Sir Alf. When England failed to qualify for the 1974 World Cup, again in somewhat crazy circumstances with the Polish goalkeeper Tomaszewski performing his miracles at Wembley, England's greatest manager was sacked. His own description of it makes grim reading: 'It was the most devastating half hour of my life,' he said later. 'I stood in a room almost full of staring commitee men. It was just like I was on trial. I thought I was going to be hanged.'

It was only much later that the scale of his achievements was appreciated, not just for 1966 but for the way that England played in Mexico too. On the day that it all started to go wrong, against West Germany, the opposition contained at least two players – Uwe Seeler and Gerd Müller – who are now ranked among the greats of European football, and another, Franz Beckenbauer, who was a bit more than that.

West Germany's preparation for Mexico had involved a game against Ireland in Berlin. I played in that game, in which Seeler scored the only goal. I don't think they were killing themselves on the day. It was just a bit of a run-out for them. Seeler had been a leading light in German football for years, the captain in 1966 and 1970. He was a terrific centre-forward, with great technique, and he was quick. For a smallish sort of a guy – he was not much bigger than me – he was brilliant in the air. He headed that late equaliser against England in León. Seeler was the first player ever to score in four World Cups, and the only one to score at least two goals in each of them. But as if to show that the stars of German football were no more financially secure than their British counterparts, it is also on the record that the great Uwe Seeler played a match for Cork Celtic in the League of Ireland, a route that had also been taken by George Best and Geoff Hurst. Seeler lined out for Cork Celtic in 1978, in a one-off sponsored event that was also a regular League of Ireland fixture. He scored twice in a 6–2 defeat of Shamrock Rovers.

Seeler officially retired in 1972, but striker Gerd Müller would go on to win the European Championship with West Germany in 1972 and the World Cup in 1974, scoring the winning goal in the final that was typical of his finishing style – receiving the ball in the box and then creating the space with his first touch before turning it into the net with acute awareness of all the angles.

In León, he stuck a dagger into the heart of England with the winning goal in extra time. The ball had been crossed to the far post and headed back across the six-yard box, for Müller to bang it into the net with Bonetti again unable to intervene. Müller was the leading scorer with ten goals in that tournament, in which West Germany did not reach the final even after their heroics against England and then Italy.

I played against him for Leeds, when we were beaten by Bayern Munich in the 1975 European Cup final, by which time he had been well established as one of the best out-and-out goal scorers that has ever been seen. Seeler was probably a better player all round than Müller, but Müller had that special gift, that genius of the finisher. Again he was a short fellow, with a similar type of build to, say, Kevin Phillips, the former Sunderland striker. He was strong, with a low centre of gravity. Very few could turn as quickly as he did, whipping in shots, especially on his right side. He was particularly strong when he had his back to goal, with that excellent positional sense of his. He knew when to go to the near post, when to make a sprint, to pull away from the centre-half, all those instincts of the natural goal scorer. It is a role as specialised as that of the goalkeeper who, like the finisher, is not involved much in the game overall but who has a unique responsibility.

John Aldridge, for example, was an ugly duckling outside the box, but a glorious swan inside it. Müller might have been a bit more accomplished than John, but they both knew that all great play had to be finished off, and that they were the men to do it. When the Liverpool team under Kenny Dalglish in 2011–2012 complained that 'we made loads of chances but we couldn't score', you got a sense of the crucial importance of an Aldridge or an Ian Rush or a Jimmy Greaves or a Gerd Müller. If you put Müller into an ordinary team, he would still score a fair number of goals. But most strikers, even in a very good team, wouldn't score as many as Müller did.

Apart from the three goal scorers against England – Beckenbauer, Seeler and Müller – that German team of 1970 had several excellent players such as Karl-Heinz Schnellinger, who played at full-back for them for years, Berti Vogts who was very, very good, Wolfgang Overath on the left side of midfield and Sepp Maier in goal.

But it was Franz Beckenbauer who would eventually be seen as the greatest of all the Germans, and one of the greatest in the history of the game. In 1966, he had played for West Germany in midfield, and had marked Bobby Charlton in the final. In 1970, he was still playing in midfield and scoring goals, and displaying his indomitable character in the semi-final against Italy, when he was fouled and fell awkwardly, dislocating his shoulder. He played the rest of the match and on through extra time with his arm and shoulder strapped up – 'Not able to give 100 per cent,' as he said later – but still a presence on the pitch. The West Germans had already made their two substitutions which was the maximum allowed – a progressive development as this was the first World Cup at which subsitutes were allowed at all – and the game against Italy was becoming one of those crazy epics, finishing 1–1 in normal time after a late equaliser by Schnellinger for the Germans, with the Italians eventually winning it 4–3. They were different times back then, in terms of health and safety, but even by 1970 standards, the decision of Beckenbauer to stay on the pitch with a dislocated shoulder was impressive.

With his elegant style of play, Beckenbauer was always being compared to Bobby Moore, whose World Cup on this occasion he had helped to end. As we have seen, Moore also started out in midfield before moving back into defence, and because he and Beckenbauer were players of real ability, it became easier for them when they moved back, because then they could see everything in front of them. They read it so well, and their technique enabled them to control the ball brilliantly, which meant that they could have a huge influence in the game. But I think that Beckenbauer had the edge on Moore.

He was much quicker than Bobby, and of course he was challenging for all the major trophies throughout his career, leaving no time for the boredom that would sometimes creep into Bobby's spirit in the weekly routine at West Ham. When I played against Beckenbauer in that European Cup final of 1975, I learned at first hand that if you got too close to him, he could just go past you. So in deference to his speed and skill, you had to concede him a certain amount of space, which enabled him to look up and to release the ball effectively. Very effectively. If you did not concede him that space, he would dribble past you. From his point of view, it was heads I win, tails you lose. Football is all about time and space, and Beckenbauer was the master of both. When you had him on the team, it was like having two players instead of one – two very good players at that. Because after moving up the pitch and distributing the ball, he could get back to resume his position as a defender. It was like having a player in the middle of the field who could distribute the ball, but who was still able to operate as a full-time sweeper.

By the time we played them in 1975, Bayern Munich with Beckenbauer, Müller and Uli Hoeness were in the second year of their three-year period as holders of the European Cup. And Beckenbauer had that aura of a great player but, for a long time in that game, we were better than them – Beckenbauer's foul on Allan Clarke in the first half was obviously a penalty but was not given. And the referee disallowed a goal by Peter Lorimer – offside was given against Billy Bremner – when the match was still scoreless in the second half. Bayern scored soon afterwards and won the match 2–0.

Beckenbauer may not have dominated that game, but he was brilliant in it. He dominated many of the games in which he played and ultimately he influenced the game as a whole, with his undeniable greatness. So many of his opponents over the years must have faced that dilemma – do you get close to him and just watch him run past you, or do you give him the space which will have roughly the same effect? Like all the great players, on the field he gave you two choices when you came up against him – a bad choice and a terrible choice. The rest was up to you.

8

The Masters

By the time the top countries of Europe had exhausted one another in the terrible heat and the altitude of Mexico, it was left to Brazil to win the 1970 World Cup. Not that they would have been denied, no matter where the finals had been held. I am always a bit wary of describing any team as the best team ever, but certainly that Brazilian team would be up there. You can only be the best of your time, and Brazil in 1970 were certainly the best of theirs.

These guys played football, really brilliant football, relating to one another all the time, their technique immaculate and Pelé at his best. I've already mentioned Jairzinho, but all these guys could play. Gerson was left-footed, with beautiful control and vision, not unlike Xavi at Barcelona. Tostão was another left-footed lad, a little fellow, small and pale and not very athletic-looking, but like all great players he gave the impression that the ball was stuck to him. Again I think of Xavi and Iniesta and Messi at Barcelona, who also have that quality.

Tostão was always playing little one-twos, relating to everyone around him, knowing when to hold the ball, when to deliver it, when to get it back. That is what creates the magic, the understanding that these players had of each other as individuals and collectively. Some call it samba football, but that always sounds a bit like bullshit to me. These guys were just master footballers. Such was their control of the ball and their ability to manoeuvre, that they would build up this grace and rhythm that was so attractive – bringing someone else into the game by playing a ball to his feet, scoring goals, it was a marvellous sight but it was also effective. You often hear it said that two players can't play in the same team because, even though both are excellent, 'their styles are too similar'. That is nonsense, because by definition an excellent player should always be able to relate to another excellent player, and that is what these guys did – it's the less than excellent ones you have to watch out for.

These fellows could all play. The full-back Carlos Alberto scored that famous goal in the final when he completed a movement which had involved most of the Brazil team by running on to Pelé's perfectly weighted ball and striking it perfectly into the bottom corner of the net. It came as no surprise that he could do that – which in itself was surprising.

A few years later, I played against Carlos Alberto in America, where he was playing for the New York Cosmos and I was with the Philadelphia Furies. He was older than me, getting towards the end of his career, but he was brilliant. And, of course, I was in the Azteca Stadium in 1970 when he scored the fourth goal against Italy in the final, that last flourish of this wonderful Brazil side. The happy travelling party of the Great Britain eleven and their eleven companions had been taken to Acapulco after the group stages to unwind, but we were back in Mexico City for the final. I remember that the seating arrangements at the huge stadium were chaotic, the result of what seemed like dubious ticketing practices – basically you just took the first seat you could get, because the one you were supposed to be in had already gone. It is certainly a long way from there to the tightly controlled corporate arrangements of today.

There were over 100,000 people in the stadium, with no stewarding, but somehow we got a good view of the match. Though we reckoned that England or West Germany would have given Brazil a better game than Italy did. They were definfitely tired, but they were not the best of the European teams. Certainly the Italian league at the time was regarded as the best, or at least the richest. The move by a top player, such as Luis Suárez Miramontes from Barcelona to Inter Milan in the 1960s was regarded as a step up for him.

But looking back, the Italian national side did not have the great players that England or West Germany had. The captain Giacinto Facchetti was a world-class full-back. And Gianni Rivera was the idol of AC Milan, but I thought he was a bit of a pretty boy. I don't think he could stand up to a lot of physical stuff. He played for Milan against Leeds United in the 1973 Cup Winners' Cup final in Thessalonika, a match that I missed through injury, and which Milan won 1–0 after a completely bizarre display by the referee. Rivera was a good player, an out-and-out midfielder, but I have those reservations about him. He wasn't even in the starting eleven for the World Cup final because of a school of thought in the Italian camp that said that he and Sandro Mazzola couldn't play together. Here we are again, with this theory that 'their styles are too similar', but I suspect the truth was different. I don't think that Rivera and Mazzola got on personally, maybe something to do with Rivera being the top man at AC Milan and Mazzola having the same status at Inter Milan.

Mazzola was more of a striker than a midfield player, so you wouldn't have thought his style and that of Rivera would be too similar. Anyway I feel that Luigi Riva was better than either of them. Perhaps he was not as big a name as the idols of Milan – he played for Cagliari – and he was not what we regard as a typical Italian player. Riva was very direct, strong, a left-winger roughly in the style of James McClean today. He was good in the air and he scored a lot of goals, but not against Brazil on that day.

The first goal for Brazil, of course, was headed in by Pelé from a cross by Rivelino. I never played against Pelé, but I played against Brazil twice and, through that, learned something of what he meant to the other players. The first time I played against them was at Lansdowne Road in 1973 for the Shamrock Rovers All-Ireland team that featured players from the North and the Republic, a selection which consisted of Pat Jennings, Derek Dougan, Terry Conroy, Bryan Hamilton, Miah Dennehy, Liam O'Kane, Mick Martin, Don Givens, Allan Hunter, Paddy Mulligan, Tommy Carroll, Tommy Craig and Martin O'Neill. It was, I think, a great day for Ireland all round, even though we were beaten 4–3 by a Brazilian team that still had Jairzinho, Rivelino and Paulo Cesar, but no Pelé, Tostão or Gerson, who had all retired. The following year, as manager of the Republic, we went to Brazil to play them as part of their preparation for the 1974 World Cup – the late Louis Kilcoyne, then head of the FAI, was able to arrange it and the All-Ireland game through his friendship with João Havelange, the Brazilian who was to become the President of FIFA in 1974. And in that friendly at the Maracana, which we lost 2–1, they were delighted that we gave them a good, open game, unlike their other warm-up opponents who played very defensively. As a gesture, they invited me to spend a bit of time with them at their World Cup training camp in Frankfurt.

Talking to Rivelino in particular about Pelé, I realised how much the other players loved him. Which is not always the way with the star man, who can sometimes dominate all around him, inhibiting other players who are in awe of him. Pelé was one of those stars who are liked by their colleagues as much as they are revered, which is not just a good thing in itself, but which will tend to bring the best out of all around him. This is a key to understanding his greatness. Everything he did was for the team. He was a senior player in 1970, no longer the prodigy that we had first seen in those black-and-white glimpses from Sweden in 1958. In fact, there had been some trouble in the Brazil camp in the run-up to Mexico, with an unpopular manager being replaced by Mario Zagallo, so they needed the leadership of Pelé, and he was not found wanting. The respect and affection in which he was held by the likes of Rivelino – a great player himself – confirmed to me that Pelé was the ultimate pro.

That is why he was the best. We know that he was a leading light, with great ability, but that could be said of others who did not have Pelé's professionalism, his modesty and humility. You never saw him having a go at another player, remonstrating with him. Always if the simple ball was on, he would play it. He would pick up the ball and do his stuff, with no stupid tricks. And if something a bit less simple was required, of course he was able to do that too.

In the group stages in Mexico, when Pelé tried to lob the Czechoslovakian keeper with a shot from inside his own half, he was not just showing off, he was taking the best option that he had at the time. And he very nearly scored. When he sold that outrageous dummy to the Uruguay keeper in the semi-final, then chased after the ball in the area and turned it narrowly wide, that too was the best option. It was not a 'trick', as I have seen it described. These guys could shimmy, but not just for the sake of it. Doing the spectacular thing is perfectly all right if it is effective and the best thing for the team. Often you just see it being done to please the crowd, but that would be alien to Pelé.

Scoring the opening goal in the 1970 final with a great header, making the breakthrough against the Italian defence, was typical. He did it when it mattered. He had that perfect combination of great talent and great attitude, and the Brazilian team as a whole was infused by it, always attacking when they could, as attractive as they were effective. This is what people really want to see on the pitch, and this team led by Pelé brought it to a new level, establishing a style that we call 'typically Brazilian'. I don't think you needed to be from Brazil to play it – Bobby Charlton or George Best could have played for that Brazil team – and we have seen Brazilian teams led by Dunga, for example, which are not 'typically Brazilian' at all. But whatever we want to call it, we didn't realise how great it could be until Pelé, Rivelino, Jairzinho, Gerson, Tostão and Carlos Alberto seized their moment, put it all together and showed us.

The Netherlands were not in Mexico in 1970, but Dutch football in general was emerging as a phenomenon at the time. Like Brazil, the Dutch teams were playing in a way that was both very attractive and highly effective. But it all happened very quickly.

In Leeds United's early seasons in Europe, we regarded any Dutch team as a joke. They were amateurs, really, and hopeless all round. The next thing we knew, in 1966–1967, this team called Ajax were beating Liverpool 7–3 on aggregate in the European Cup. They had won the first leg in Amsterdam 5–1, though there was heavy fog on the night, which gave the Kop – and probably Bill Shankly himself – the hope that this was a freak result and that Liverpool would destroy them at Anfield. But Ajax, whose very name had been regarded as a joke by Liverpool fans given that it was the same name as a toilet cleaner, managed a 2–2 draw. Both goals were scored by some guy called Johan Cruyff.

Clearly, when they were turning professional, the Dutch football administrators had got a lot of things right and had gone about it in the most enlightened way. This was such a rare thing in the overall context of football administration, it can probably be counted as a miracle in itself. I have found the Dutch in general to be very intelligent and practical people, and this is borne out by the way they improved their football so dramatically. Starting from scratch, the most important thing that they got right was the coaching. Clearly they brought in the right people, because not only has that coaching stayed with them ever since, they have exported it. They would also avoid all the nonsense about freedom of contract and the maximum wage which had blighted the British game, and that more progressive mindset was mirrored in the way that they played football.

Maybe the very nature of Holland itself, in which every square inch of space is important, was a good influence in terms of football, which itself is all about creating space. Whatever it was, they were suddenly beating the best teams in England, and showing clubs like Liverpool what they needed to do to succeed in Europe – an amazing transformation. Ajax reached the final of the European Cup in 1969, where they were beaten by AC Milan. But when a Dutch team won the European Cup for the first time in 1970, it was not Ajax but Feyenoord who did it. Though Ajax would then do it for the next three years.

Feyenoord beat the outstanding Celtic team that had beaten Leeds in the semi-final that year, the Feyenoord winner coming a few minutes from the end of extra-time in the San Siro, after a 1–1 draw in normal time. And though everyone knew by now that Dutch football was no longer a joke, or anything like it, that first big win still came as a surprise. Soon, under the leadership of Cruyff, it would be a surprise for a Dutch team not to win the European Cup.

Cruyff was a truly brilliant player, up there with the greats. He was quick, with good control, and he could do it on his own. And as for his confidence, let us say that Johan Cruyff didn't suffer from an inferiority complex. He was not scared of it. To this day, Cruyff has a lot to say for himself, but then it might be added that he is a man worth listening to, because along with all his achievements in the game for Ajax and the Netherlands, he is also credited with introducing Barcelona to its current philosophy. The basics were established in that excellent Dutch coaching system, with the result that the technique of all the players was excellent, from the full-backs all the way through the team. And after that, they applied themselves well.

Without the hang-ups of the more subservient British players, they also had an independence about them, an ability to think for themselves. This was a great asset in terms of believing in the way that they played, in keeping the ball and not resorting to more stupid methods under pressure. But it could be a disadvantage when it came to major championships, when the Dutch seemed to be forever in the throes of some crisis about bonuses or about bringing their wives or about the coffee not being warm enough in the morning. In these situations, maybe a few of those old-style British hang-ups might have saved them a lot of trouble.

Just as quickly as they had arrived on the scene, the papers were describing what the Dutch were doing as 'total football'. They love a label. The Tottenham team of the early 1950s managed by Arthur Rowe became the 'push and run' team, whatever that was supposed to mean. Certainly they were a very attractive team, in their own way, who passed the ball very well, but 'push and run' is another of those strangely meaningless terms that doesn't really stand up to scrutiny – a bit like 'getting more men in the box' and 'bombing forward'. Push and run is all very well, but sometimes when you push the ball, the best thing to do is not to run. Sometimes there is nowhere to run to, and you are better off standing still. Or even moving backwards.

There was another reason why I didn't really subscribe to the 'total football' label being put on the Dutch, and on their national team in particular, and that was because I thought we were already doing it at Leeds.

We had Terry Cooper and Paul Reaney at full-back who would attack at every opportunity and who had the technique to play in any Dutch side. We had Eddie Gray who was an absolutely brilliant winger, a joy to watch and, like Cruyff, a player who could do it on his own. We had players throughout the team who were individually as gifted as any of their Dutch counterparts and who also had that collective desire to play in the most positive way. Probably at this stage we had been around so long and had such a bad press there was no way the media was going to turn around and start comparing us to the team that they were always calling the 'Dutch Masters'. But anyone who really knows the game would understand that in this period early in the 1970s, Leeds were playing some extraordinarily good football. And even if it was not labelled 'total football', there was a certain totality about it.

Even a really big name like Johan Neeskens could be matched by his Leeds counterpart and, to tell the truth, I would put Billy Bremner ahead of Neeskens. I always thought Neeskens was a bit of an up-and-downer. A good player, but no more than that. I wouldn't regard him as one of the real stars of Dutch football, not like Cruyff, Ruud Krol or Wim van Hanegem, and not in the same bracket either as the Dutch players who would come after him such as Ruud Gullit, Marco van Basten and Ronald Koeman. Certainly when Leeds were playing Barcelona in the semi-final of the European Cup in 1975, we weren't scared of him in any way. But as it turned out, we did not have a great deal to fear from Johan Cruyff either, over the two games.

Before the tie, all the talk was of Cruyff and Neeskens, and the new Dutch influence at Barcelona, and this was all good stuff – but we beat them 2–1 at Elland Road. Unfortunately for me, the weekend before the second leg, I got injured in a game against Ipswich Town. Jimmy Armfield was the Leeds manager by then, and I said to Jimmy that I didn't want to play against Ipswich, I needed to rest before the second leg at Camp Nou. Jimmy asked me to play anyway, and as I slid into a tackle on David Johnson, I got caught under the ribcage and broke two ribs – a very, very sore thing, by the way.

So I had a good view of Peter Lorimer making it 3–1 on aggregate at Camp Nou after seven minutes, running on to a header by Joe Jordan and blasting it into the top corner.

Barcelona equalised after seventy minutes but we felt deep down that they weren't going to get a second goal against us. And on the night, I was a bit disappointed by Cruyff. He stayed out on the wing, rather than coming into midfield a bit more to try and dictate the game from there. It was 1975, admittedly; he had been a great player since the late 1960s, and I'm not sure if he was that interested any more. In the great days, he had done most of his damage down the middle. But out on the wing, you are depending on others to get the ball out to you, which makes it much more difficult. And people know where you are, which makes it easier to keep an eye on you. In recent times, Lionel Messi has found this too, which is why he moved to the centre. Now he can chase after the ball, win it back, control it more.

Whether he was on the wing or at centre-forward, Cruyff could always do things that other players could not do. That European Cup semi-final, like the defeat to West Germany in the 1974 World Cup final, which had been the first major disappointment for Dutch fans, had come at the end of a period of dazzling achievement for Cruyff, with the three European Cups in a row with Ajax. Meanwhile the best of the Germans who played for Bayern Munich were about to replace Ajax as the dominant force in Europe, winning their own three in a row, starting in 1974.

Certainly lovers of Dutch football have always seen them as the 'moral' winners of that 1974 World Cup, and we in Ireland have a deep understanding of that, in our own way. But West Germany had also won the European Championship in 1972. And maybe in 1974, when the whole world discovered the beauty and the brilliance of Dutch football, it had already reached its peak, and now the Germans were taking over at the top.

The Netherlands were almost everybody's favourite team, but in that 1974 World Cup they were not as solid as the Germans. Basically, they were not as good. West Germany did not have the glamour but they still had terrific players. People thought they were not as attractive to watch, but I certainly found them attractive to watch. As far as I could see, those German fellows weren't exactly falling over the ball either, they all had a very good first touch. Man for man, I thought they just had the edge on the Dutch. Apart from Beckenbauer, Müller, Overath, Vogts and Maier, they had Paul Breitner, who could play either left-back or right-back, breaking a bit into midfield later on. He was good enough to play in all these positions, and he was not one-dimensional as a person either. Breitner was a bit of a hippy, not a typical footballer – he had outside interests, as it were. Maybe in temperament, he was a bit more like the Dutch players.

And one of the better German players of that generation wasn't even in the World Cup squad. Günter Netzer of Borussia Mönchengladbach was a top-class midfield player, quite a tall lad, more brilliant that Wolfgang Overath, who had a workmanlike style. I don't think Netzer was injured in 1974, so his omission was something of a mystery to me at the time. He had destroyed England at Wembley in 1972, running riot in a performance that suggested there were great things ahead for him as West Germany's main man. He had also played in the team that won the European Championship in 1972. I played against him, again at Wembley the following year, in a friendly match to celebrate the accession of Ireland, Britain and Denmark to the EEC. The match was called 'The Three Against The Six', the 'six' being the countries already in the EEC. Among the players selected for the 'three' were Pat Jennings, Bobby Moore, Emlyn Hughes, Pat Rice, Allan Hunter, Peter Lorimer, Colin Stein and Colin Bell.

Netzer was, again, outstanding. There was a story, no more than a rumour really, that Beckenbauer mightn't have wanted him in the squad for 1974 – that he felt Netzer might not be necessary, given the way that Beckenbauer himself played, coming into midfield from the back. Anyway, West Germany did it without him. And though they were not the popular choice, they deserved to do it.

9

Keegan or Dalglish?

Kevin Keegan is now mainly known as a TV pundit and a former manager who has come out with various funny lines over the years – lines that he didn't intend to be funny, like, 'Chile have three options, they could win or they could lose' or 'That would have been a goal if it wasn't saved.' As an RTÉ pundit myself, I have every sympathy for Kevin in this regard and I can only pray that the words I am saying on live television will not come back to haunt me.

But it should never be forgotten that Kevin Keegan was not just a great player, he was one of the most important players in the history of the English game. When he left Liverpool of his own volition, at a time of his choosing and for another club, also of his choosing, he broke through a psychological barrier that had held back almost every footballer in these islands, myself included. It had never crossed my mind to leave Leeds, to make the effort. Probably since the days of the Bogota rebels, the pattern had been established of players not bucking the sytem. The fate of the Bogota lads had sent a shiver down the spine of almost every footballer playing in Britain, and it would be a long time before they stood up for themselves again. During the famous George Eastham case, brought by the players' union, a judge had compared the 'retain-and-transfer' system to a form of slavery, and yet that had been forgotten, the players cleverly bought off by the removal of the maximum wage.

Not that most of them were up for a fight with their clubs anyway. Over the decades, the whole way that the game was organised had corroded the dignity of the players, made them fearful of challenging the authorities. And then Kevin Keegan, at the height of Liverpool's success in the 1970s, decided that he wanted to move to Hamburg whether Liverpool liked it or not. And with one mighty leap, our hero was free.

Kevin was a hero to me anyway for what he did. Several European clubs had wanted him, and midway through what would be his last season at Liverpool he made his announcement that he was leaving. He decided on Hamburg. The transfer fee was £500,000 and Keegan became the highest-paid player in Germany. But before saying goodbye to Liverpool in 1977, a club he geniunely loved, they won the Double of the league and the European Cup, their first of the famous five.

Kenny Dalglish, meanwhile, was bought by Liverpool from Celtic using £440,000 of the £500,000 they got for Keegan, setting a new British transfer record, but also making a tidy profit. And with Kenny, Liverpool entered an even more glorious phase, at home and in Europe. Over in Germany, Keegan went on to win the Bundesliga with Hamburg and was named European Footballer of the Year for two years in a row.

All things considered, it is hard to imagine a single move in English football history that turned out to be more beneficial for all concerned, and yet this was the scenario that had been avoided and feared for decades by more timid souls. Keegan wasn't one of them, he just wasn't made that way. In fact he was probably the perfect candidate to negotiate such a deal because he just didn't bother much with the downside of things. The qualities he brought to his transfer to Hamburg were similar to the qualities that had given him such a successful career in the first place. He had an unquenchable optimism about him, a total belief in his own ability and an absolute determination to make the most of that ability through hard work and dedication.

If Bill Shankly had been able to invent the perfect player for his vision of Liverpool, he would have ended up with someone like Kevin Keegan – all that drive and energy and passion. But Shankly didn't have to create him in a laboratory, he just went out and bought him from Scunthorpe United for £35,000. He had also bought Ray Clemence from Scunthorpe United for less than £20,000, and Clemence was already becoming one of the several great British goalkeepers of that time, proving again that by far the most important part of any manager's job is bringing the right sort of players into the club.

To bring those two in particular for £55,000 combined must rank as one of Shankly's more outrageous acts of genius. Many other managers had looked at Keegan at Scunthorpe – but only Shankly believed. There is a sheep-like thing in football, whereby if one club wants to buy a player, the rest of them start to get anxious, thinking that they must be missing something. And sometimes a young player is obviously outstanding, which makes it easy for the scouts. But the great talent-spotters can see a player in a poor team, having a terrible game, and still see something in him. They think, 'If I had him, I would make him better.' The belief is in themselves as much as in the player. And, in the case of Shankly and Keegan, that belief transformed Liverpool Football Club for the second time since Shankly became manager. The first transformation had created that powerful team of the 1960s which now needed to be replenished – something that is always a diffcult task. To create one great team is remarkable, to recreate that success with hardly a pause for breath is almost impossible, as Tottenham, Arsenal, Manchester City and of course Manchester United were proving. Even Shankly had been struggling to replenish a team which had featured the likes of Ian St John and Ron Yeats. Before Keegan arrived, it had been six years since Liverpool had won the league. In Keegan's second season at the club they had won it again, and they won the UEFA Cup too.

Which was one of the many remarkable things about Kevin Keegan. Not only was he the catalyst for what would turn out to be the most successful period in ths history of Liverpool,

he made his mark straight away. He came to the club near the
end of the 1970–1971 season, and he was in the team for the
start of the next season – not only was he in the team, he was
a star. Again, that would go back to Keegan's personality. He
had embraced the Liverpool thing as his natural destiny, never
feeling that it was too big for him, and if anything feeling that
he was better than anyone else there. Though they were very
different players in many ways, a comparison can be made to
the way Eric Cantona arrived at Manchester United thinking
that here, at last, was a stadium big enough to hold him.

At the other end of the scale, we have seen how players
such as Stewart Downing and Charlie Adam, who had done
reasonably well at smaller clubs, have tended to be diminished
by the enormity of signing for Liverpool, rarely sending out
the strong signal that 'this is where I should be'. Keegan by
contrast was a leader almost from the moment he arrived, and
under that leadership Liverpool started winning again – and
they never stopped for most of the next twenty years.

I played against him in his first season, and I was
immediately impressed. I had heard that this young fellow
had come on a fair bit, and sure enough he was strong and
fit, very confident about getting on the ball. He was what we
call a dasher, full of life, full of go. Shankly would say that
Keegan could 'drop these little grenades', getting on the ball
on the left wing, coming inside, shimmying, doing something
different. He would go at defenders and beat them with his
pace. He had a good shot in his right foot and he was a very,
very good header. He was very brave, forming that tremendous
partnership with John Toshack that seemed to sweep the ball

into the net at the Kop end when the team really needed it, not just with their combined talents, but by force of will. Having said all that, Keegan was not the finished article by any means. But he wouldn't have been sensitive to that. In fact, if Kevin Keegan had known his limitations, he wouldn't have been the player he was.

His technique was good, but not attractive. On a superficial level, for example, Glenn Hoddle looked like a better player, with his excellent technique and distribution of the ball. And yet Hoddle never delivered the way that Keegan did, because to my mind he lacked the aggression of the really top midfielders, the sharpness in tight situations. Hoddle was one of a few leading players of that time such as Trevor Francis, Trevor Brooking and Gerry Francis, who were still promising to be great players right until the end of their careers, without ever really getting there. They would quite often be described as great players by commentators and pundits, but unlike Keegan, did not fully realise the potential that everyone saw in them. They were all good players who, for one reason or another, did not march on. Trevor Francis had been a wonder boy at Birmingham City, scoring goals at the age of sixteen, the first million-pound player in Britain and a good lad in general, and yet by the time he had finished playing I still didn't know what his best position was. Trevor Brooking at West Ham could do certain things well, but he never commanded a game. He did most of his work on the right or the left, in a peripheral way. Gerry Francis at QPR was a very good player, who never quite went on to be a Graeme Souness. In their good-but-not-great way, they were the successors to players like George Eastham and Johnny 'Budgie' Byrne. There is no doubt that George Eastham at Newcastle, Arsenal and Stoke City could really play, that he could be beautiful to watch. But when it came to the physical aspect of the game, he was a bit wanting. You always felt that a hard tackle early on would keep him quiet for the rest of the game. 'Budgie' Byrne shone brightly for West Ham and for England for a short period in the mid-1960s, but he went out of it very quickly. Budgie, it must be said, liked a drink. Oddly enough, Glenn Hoddle, Trevor Brooking and Gerry Francis had a contemporary who did not receive as much attention as they did, a Scottish international who was actually very good in midfield – Bobby Hope at West Brom was never called a great player, but he played that classic midfield role, dictating the flow of a game in a way that these more celebrated names did not.

But Kevin Keegan was out there in a category of his own, a player who brushed away whatever weaknesses he had to make himself great. Nor was Keegan the brainy type of player, or at least that's how it appeared to me. Johan Cruyff, for example, was the finished article. He was sophisticated, classy, could pick out a pass. Keegan couldn't really do that. He could go past players, without having any great knowledge of doing it. There was a touch of Andy McDaft about him – and of the players in the Liverpool dressing room, I'd say that Keegan didn't have much input into the team talks. Not that he had any inhibitions, it was just the way he was – he approached the game like a kid, and no matter what the occasion, he was going to do it. I think he carried that attitude into his managerial career. He was a bandwagon guy, with a tremendous ability to generate a spirit of optimism, in which everything is great, everything is rosy and terrific, the team is going to go out and play and attack. But when you get a few bad results, it needs knowledge to turn it around. If a team loses three matches in a row, there's no point in telling them they're doing great, you have to be able to put it right.

Most players, even the great players, are conscious of what can go wrong in a game. The great players, having considered what can go wrong, still know that they can do it. Which doesn't stop them from being nervous before a game. Of course they are nervous, because every game they play they are going into the unknown, a place in which all sorts of things can go wrong. With Keegan, nothing was ever going to go wrong. And I think that that confidence finally got the better of him when he played in midfield for Hamburg against Nottingham Forest in the 1980 European Cup final. By that time, he was a hero at Hamburg as he had been at Liverpool, but here he was trying to dictate the game, and he couldn't. He was purely a forward player, and by trying to play from such a deep position, he lost his real value. He could not throw his little grenades from there, or at least, they weren't landing on the most important targets. Again, he could not see his limitations. But this time there was no advantage to it, and Hamburg lost the final 1–0 to Forest, the goal scored by John Robertson.

He still had done remarkable things in his time, not least the feat of turning Liverpool into winners again. I took a particularly keen and personal interest in that, because for a couple of seasons there was huge competition between Leeds United and Liverpool, with Leeds beating them to the league in 1974. At which point, of course, Leeds as a club proceeded to do everything wrong, while Liverpool kept on doing everything right.

The signing of Kenny Dalglish was just one of those things. I think Kenny was one of the great players. But if I was picking a team, I would genuinely find it hard to have Dalglish in there instead of Keegan. Kenny undoubtedly looked the classier player – and that wasn't just a superficial thing, because he actually was classier – and the Liverpool fans will always probably place him ahead of Keegan in their affections – Keegan left them, after all – yet I don't think that Keegan has quite received the recognition to which he is entitled for what he did for that club. So if you're asking me to pick a team, and I'm choosing between Dalglish and Keegan as to who will have the most overall effect, I would find it really hard to separate the two. That is how highly I would rate Keegan.

I'd have a lot of time for him too, on a personal level. Kevin was one of the few football people, apart from the Leeds lads, to attend the funeral of Don Revie in Edinburgh in 1989. Keegan had played for Don when Don was manager of England. And while the FA did not acknowledge Don's passing in any way, Kevin made the journey to pay his respects.

Bill Shankly had predeceased Don Revie by eight years. In his unhappy retirement, he had seen Liverpool become the dominant force in British and European football, and his successor Bob Paisley get much of the credit. But really, to compare Shankly and Paisley is to compare apples and oranges. Paisley did brilliantly for Liverpool. He was very wise and very good to have the intelligence not to put his stamp on what was there already, as lesser men might have done. He lacked that sort of destructive ego. He was not thinking, 'I'll build my team' but 'I am taking over Bill's team.'

Having said that, there is no way that Bob Paisley could have done what Shankly did. It is much easier to continue success than to create it. Let us not forget that Paisley was at Liverpool before Shankly, and I didn't see any great team emerging at that time. He was also fortunate given the disintegration of Leeds and the decline of Manchester United, leaving Liverpool with no serious challengers until Brian Clough's Nottingham Forest came along in the late 1970s. The Derby County team that had won the league in 1975 under Dave Mackay turned out to be a one-season wonder. Clough had built that team of Roy McFarland, Colin Todd, Archie Gemmill, Alan Durban, Kevin Hector and Alan Hinton, and they might have been able to sustain a challenge in the longer term if it wasn't for the departure of Clough. As it was, Liverpool just kept on going, troubled only by teams like QPR finishing in second.

Not that the weaknesses of others should take away from Paisley's achievements in this great period. Liverpool could only do their own thing, and let the others look after themselves. And they did their own thing wonderfully well. The replenishing that had started under Shankly continued, with Kenny Dalglish emerging as a great player, leading one of the great teams. Kenny was technically brilliant. His knowledge and his positional sense were also brilliant. And he was a real pro.

What Dalglish did might sound simple – playing just off the centre-forward, acting as the link between the midfield and

Ian Rush who played very far forward – but it involved getting the ball, holding it, making the right pass, creating goals, scoring goals. It was different to what Keegan had done, and the subsequent addition of Graeme Souness brought a further dimension to Liverpool, one that had actually never been there in the entire time of Shankly. Souness was a genuinely creative midfield player. Despite all their success, Liverpool had never had an out-and-out midfield 'general'. Going back, the role of Ian St John had been a bit like that of Dalglish. Players like Gordon Milne, Willie Stevenson and Geoff Strong were good all-round midfield players, but none of them were generals. Emlyn Hughes, Peter Cormack, Ian Callaghan, Ray Kennedy and Sammy Lee were all important players but, again, none of them were generals in the middle of midfield.

I think Graeme Souness was a great player, and coming just after Dalglish, he was a hugely influential signing. Maybe not quite as influential as Keegan had been, but he still made a dramatic change to the team. Again, Liverpool was not too big a club for Graeme. He was ready for it. He had left Spurs, unhappy that he was not making enough progress, and gone to Middlesbrough where he had established himself and had time to mature. I played against him twice at Boro. He was young, aggressive and his overall contribution was excellent. If there was one slight thing against him, it was his lack of that extra bit of pace. Graeme wasn't quick. If he was to ask the gods for one little thing more, that would be it, but his distribution was excellent and he had the confidence and the ability to dominate a game. He was a player with that mysterious thing called presence – in other words, a leader.

Liverpool were already starting to dominate, and the signing of Souness made sure that they continued to dominate. Because Souness had a rough-and-ready aspect to him, perhaps he doesn't get the credit that he deserves. Yet it is clear to me that he made a real difference. Whenever Leeds were up against the old Shankly-type of midfield player, the energetic all-action ones, I always felt that we had the upper hand. With myself, Billy Bremner and Eddie Gray in the middle, there was a dimension to us that Liverpool lacked. With Souness against us, we might not have had the upper hand any more.

Through the spine of the team, they now had Alan Hansen, Souness, Dalglish and Ian Rush – and for a long time, no one would have the upper hand on that side.

Liverpool and Rush were also made for each other, showing again that you need someone with that killer instinct to get the goals, to finish off all that good play. Hansen was a different class. He was one of the quickest players I have seen, deceptively so in the manner of Beckenbauer. He had that same easy loping stride that Beckenbauer had, a real footballer who played at the back but who had the creative mind of a midfielder.

Just behind the legendary pair of Dalglish and Souness, I would place Steve Nicol, another terrific player for Liverpool who tends to be mentioned only in passing, the way that Tony Dunne and Shay Brennan were overshadowed by the Manchester United immortals of the 1960s. If Nicol is behind Dalglish and Souness, it is not by much. He was a highly valuable player, who could play full-back or midfield, and give a good account of himself anywhere. A top-class player.

Phil Thompson and Mark Lawrenson were also wonderful players. Tommy Smith and John Toshack were still around as late as 1978, when the European Cups started to roll in, and Ronnie Whelan had arrived on the scene. They had become a phenomenon.

Brian Clough was already a phenomenon, and not just in his own mind. Perhaps it was his own unrealised potential as a player that drove him to achieve the amazing things that he did – Clough had scored over 250 goals for Middlesbrough and Sunderland until a cruciate knee injury effectively ended his career at the age of twenty-seven. Perhaps that gave him some sort of a key to understanding the unrealised potential in the players and the teams he would manage. But that is only guesswork, as it must be whenever we are talking about a genius.

Without knowing anything about the inner workings of the mind of Brian Clough, you only have to state the main facts of his career – the league titles he won with Derby County and Nottingham Forest, with whom he also won the European Cup twice – to know that he must have been some kind of a genius. And yet in football even a man of the most unique abilities can't do it entirely on his own. The role of his assistant Peter Taylor in identifying the right players for Clough is now well known and rightly appreciated. But there was another man already at Forest when Clough arrived, who made a contribution to his successs which has not been rightly appreciated.

John Robertson had actually been at Forest since he came down from Scotland in 1970. He had looked an average player, a winger who was on the transfer list when Clough arrived at the club in 1975. According to Clough himself, Roberstson seemed unfit, overweight and uninterested, and hardly looked like a professional sportsman at all. Being Clough, he exaggerated somewhat the extent of Roberston's physical failings, but it seems clear that at the very least, Robertson had been lacking in confidence and generally insecure about his abilities. That was about to change.

Clough said that something about this unattractive young man persuaded him to keep believing in him. And apparently that is all that Roberston needed to turn himself very quickly from being a very ordinary-looking player in a very ordinary club in the East Midlands to a world-class player with the champions of Europe. Not that he would necessarily have responded in the way that he did if some other manager had had such faith in him. This was Brian Clough bestowing his blessing, and for some reason that no one will ever fully understand, when Brian Clough bestowed his blessing on a player, the results could be truly staggering. It was Clough's special power, this gift he had for making a player really want to play for him, to please him. Even when he withheld his blessing, the players craved it to such an extent that they would strive to please him anyway, in the hope that one day they might receive it. Martin O'Neill, for example, who played so well for Clough during his most successful years at Forest, says that he never fully received that blessing – but that he kept trying until the very end to get it.

So Clough might take a different approach with certain players. Martin was more of a rebellious type than John Robertson, so Clough must have felt that this was the way to get the best out of him – it was the same principle adopted to suit the personality of the player. And in the end it had the same result, with Clough getting the best out of O'Neill as he was getting the best out of Roberstson, and even out of the likes of Larry Lloyd and Kenny Burns who had reputations for being trouble-makers. It is called man-management, and all the great managers have it, though they might go about it in completely different ways – by bullying, by cajoling, by being a total bastard or a nice guy. Clough's persona was that of an arrogant fucker, but he was not just acting superior, he really felt superior. Certainly he felt superior to Kenny Burns and Larry Lloyd, who might have been giving cheek to other managers but who knew that it could never work with this guy.

If you were at the same table as Clough at a function, he would have to dominate everyone from the start. But once you deferred to him, it was fine, and then he would be building you up. A similar process was at work with the players at Forest, who would say that when Clough was building them up, they would feel ten feet tall. Now they had that blessing that they wanted so badly.

Though, of course, the blessing could only work if the player had some ability in the first place. And John Roberston, as it turned out, had the most uncommon ability. Clough spoke of him as a great artist, a Picasso, and this much is sure – Robertson became the most influential winger I have ever seen. Certainly no other winger that I am aware of could influence a game as much as he could. It is, after all, very difficult to have such a major influence from that position. Usually a winger has to rely on the midfield players to give him the ball in the first place. It is the midfield players who are dictating the pace of the game, with the winger at best embellishing what they do. But Robertson, because of his positional sense, brought a different dimension to the game.

In general, coaches make too little of the vital importance of positional sense. And yet if you don't have it, you can't use whatever ability you possess. Robertson had such a brilliant positional sense, he could get into positions on the left wing that made him seem like a magnet for the ball. And when he received it, he was able to use it in the way that a great midfield player would, so that he controlled the game from the wing rather than the middle of the field. I have never seen anyone else do that before or since. When he received the ball, Robertson used it beautifully. And when he found himself twenty yards from the by-line, as a right-footed player on the left wing, he could take defenders on, creating and scoring goals. Famously, he received the ball on the left and beat two Malmö defenders before sending a cross to the far post with his left foot for Trevor Francis to score in the 1979 European Cup final in Munich. He did that a lot over the years. And, of course, beating defenders and crossing the ball is the traditional job of the winger, except that Robertson was also doing the most important job of all – he was dictating the play. Like Beckenbauer or Hansen in their way, Robertson had become two players in one. I think, too, of Paul Scholes, who in the earlier part of his career scored a lot of goals for Manchester United, more than a creative midfield player normally would. With Scholes and Robertson in your team, it would be like having thirteen players.

Football is ultimately about common sense, about all the

players competing for space and time. The more time you have, the more you can see, and the more you can do. There is no point in having a lot of ability if you can't create the space in which to use it. So if the ball was on the opposite side of the pitch from him, you would usually see Robertson in a position about a yard behind it, rather than ten or twelve yards ahead of it, as is more common with wingers. Because Robertson was always behind the ball in this situation, when the ball came to him he could see everything in front of him, so he could take it forward or take it back, with the inside of his foot or the outside; he had all the options.

At Forest, the role he played was particularly important because they didn't have a really creative midfield player. Archie Gemmill was a very good player, but Archie was essentially a dribbler rather than a distributor. John McGovern and Ian Bowyer were quite average players – but all they had to do was give the ball to Robertson, which was an easy thing to do given the positions he would take up, and he did the creative work for them. With this great player in the side – and Peter Shilton in goal and Trevor Francis being signed for about a million – Nottingham Forest did not quite put a halt to Liverpool's gallop, but they interrupted it for a while, with that one league title in 1977–1978, the year after they were promoted, and those two European Cups in 1979 and 1980, with a couple of League Cups along the way. Apart from delivering that cross for Trevor Francis in the 1979 final, Robertson also scored the winner against Kevin Keegan's Hamburg team in 1980.

Yet I recently came across an article in which this great player was described as 'lugubrious'. Certainly Robertson did

The signing that changed everything: Keegan's brilliance was
the catalyst for Liverpool's renewed success.

Kenny Dalglish, an all-time great
and one of the few players in the
world who could replace Keegan.

Pelé, the original world superstar.

Pat Jennings. Made a difficult job look easy.

Jairzinho: one of the best players I have ever seen.

Johan Cruyff, the first of the Dutch greats.

Franz Beckenbauer: aptly nicknamed 'The Kaiser'

Diego Maradona, the Messi of his day.

Paolo Maldini, classical Italian defender.

Bryan Robson. Top-class attitude, top-class player.

Paul Scholes. After 15 years, still the best English-born midfielder.

(l to r) Frank Rijkaard, Marco Van Basten, Ruud Gullit. Worthy successors to the Cruyff legacy.

Thierry Henry and Zinedine Zidane. Brilliant players and keys to France's success.

Another great Newcastle Number
Nine, Alan Shearer.

Ryan Giggs, one of the great servants to Manchester United football club.

Steven Gerrard, a modern midfield player.

Lionel Messi, rightly acknowledged as the best player in the world.

Xavi Hernandez, understated but world-class.

not have film-star looks – he was short and a bit dumpy – but in football terms, he had star quality. In his effectiveness, he was one of the best I've ever seen. And still you can see him coming in at sixty-third in a magazine list of the hundred greatest players of all time. Given his 'lugubrious' nature, it is hard to know whether to be appalled by such a low ranking or relieved that he made it in there at all. It is a thing that annoys me greatly about football, the way that a David Beckham will always be put ahead of a Robertson, mainly because he is a celebrity. And I hasten to add that Beckham is brilliant at being a celebrity, and I have nothing against him. He was also a good player. But to say the least, he was no John Robertson.

The media never really understood how good Robertson was, but I can tell you who did – the players at Forest, who were individually not in the same class as Dalglish, Hansen, Souness, Rush or Nicol, but who had one player on their side who was most certainly in that class. And that, along with the magic of Clough, was enough.

10

Maradona
and the Curse of POMO

After winning the World Cup with Argentina in 1978, Ossie
Ardiles and Ricky Villa were signed by Tottenham Hotspur. It
was an original move and it turned out to be very successful,
giving just a taste of foreign influence, which was almost non-
existent back then but is now everywhere in the Premier League.
Ricky Villa scored the famous winner against Manchester City
in the 1981 FA Cup final, but, overall, his career with Spurs
wouldn't have encouraged an influx of players from abroad.
Ardiles was different. He was a real midfield player, small in
stature but with beautiful technique that meant that his size

didn't matter – his opponents couldn't get near him. Probably he wouldn't have been considered tough enough for the game in England if he hadn't played so well for Argentina in 1978, but he had already proved himself in that department. He had good feet, he would look up when he had the ball, and was able to relate in a football sense to those around him. I would say that Ossie Ardiles could play in the Spain team of today, which is about as high as you can set the bar.

At Ipswich Town, too, there was a very successful addition of foreign talent with the arrival of the Dutch players Arnold Muhren and Frans Thijssen. Bobby Robson had been able to build a very good team there during the 1970s with players such as Kevin Beattie, Mick Mills, Allan Hunter, Trevor Whymark, John Wark, Brian Talbot and Paul Mariner, who was a very good striker, but I always felt they were a bit short in midfield. The two Dutch guys made a big difference, bringing some extra class and creativity and making them into a top team. Ipswich still somehow never won the league, but they won the UEFA Cup in 1981 to add to the FA Cup they had won in 1978.

It now seemed like a good idea to bring in players from other countries, other football cultures, but there were a lot of bad ideas going around too, and perhaps the worst one was a thing they called POMO – the Position of Maximum Opportunity. Its main advocate was a man by the name of Charles Hughes, director of coaching at the FA. And it was the plague of football in England in the 1980s and beyond. Based on a statistical analysis – and we know statistics can prove anything you want them to prove – it suggested that the more often you got the ball into the box, the more often you would score. So you should get the ball forward as quickly as possible, into the POMO. With the emphasis on set plays and crosses, Hughes has been 'credited' with the rise of the long-ball game played to the hilt by teams like Wimbledon. The long ball is often mistaken for the long pass – there is nothing wrong with the long pass, some of the best passes ever delivered have been long passes. The difference is that the long pass actually requires some vision and some accuracy and, if it is done right, it is more effective than any long ball punted up the pitch. So Hughes was wrong about that, but he was even wrong in his use of statistics.

In fact more goals were scored as a result of good play, than by hoofing it into the box. More goals were scored when a player delivered the ball into the box after good play, with the ball coming from the right angle, than from any number of long throw-ins. And as we have seen, the great teams and the great players will often be content to wait until the right moment – they might only get the ball into the box once, but that will be enough.

But the curse of POMO was out there, and soon we were seeing fellows kicking the ball into the box from unbelievable distances. It was all about the long ball and the dead ball, which suited the Wimbledon-type of player, and bred many more of them. When it was broken down, all you needed was a goalkeeper who could kick it a long way, two big centre-halves and two big forwards up front, to combat one another. You did not need knowledge, wit or imagination – the things that make this wonderful game of ours what it is.

A midfielder wouldn't look for the ball, because when the

full-back had it, he would give it to the keeper to kick it out – in the 1980s, we must remember that the keeper could still take a back-pass and pick the ball up, bounce it around for a while wasting time, before launching it towards the sky. So the midfielder would be getting back into position for this, with the result that twenty players would congregate in the middle of the park. Then the kick-out would arrive and there would be a contest which they would call 'winning the second ball'. It was completely sterile. The midfield players would knock it backwards or forwards or it would go loose somewhere and you might get a corner kick.

So we should be eternally grateful for the introduction after Italia '90 of the back-pass rule, which meant that the keeper could no longer handle the ball when it was kicked back to him, a move which was not just good for the game in general, it had the unintentional side-effect of saving English football from itself. And I don't think that is overstating it. The game in England was transformed by this new rule. It was brought in to stop time-wasting, but by a happy accident it also made the Vinnie Joneses of this world obsolete. With the keeper unable to bounce the ball a few times and to gather his thoughts before hoofing it up the field, the midfield players didn't have the time to congregate in the middle of the pitch. Now they had to play.

But with the old rule still in place in the 1980s, Wimbledon were doing famously well, and Watford also did well, coming second in the league under Graham Taylor, which was an achievement in itself. I realise that every manager must do his best with whatever he is given. But I still don't have to like it.

You could now play the game and be quite successful without any true midfield players and, sure enough, very few people could name three or four midfielders who played for Watford in those years. They remember John Barnes on the wing, and that's about it. Bobby Charlton at his best, in fact, would have been surplus to requirements in a lot of English teams of the 1980s. Vinnie Jones became a 'character', the dreadful carry-on of Wimbledon was celebrated, even glorified in the media. I would make a distinction here between Wimbledon and Watford, because there was an honesty about Watford. They weren't known for the sort of behaviour that gave Wimbledon the reputation of being the great 'party-poopers'. But then, who would want to be a party-pooper? Nobody bothered to ask such questions, because it all seemed to be going so well for the advocates of this 'direct' style, the POMO men.

The football men of Liverpool still maintained their superiority, and Manchester United stuck to their principles in these dark times too. But eventually even Liverpool were beaten in the FA Cup final by Wimbledon.

You could see the mark of POMO in the style of play adopted by clubs as distinguished as Arsenal under George Graham and Leeds United under Howard Wilkinson. It may have been easy to do, but it was not so easy to watch. In fact at Elland Road one day, when Leeds were playing Sheffield United, there was a moment when both linesmen had their flags up for offside. It seems physically impossible, and yet it came about as a perfectly natural consequence of the way the game was going. With both teams playing offside, Leeds had knocked it forward, which led to the first offside decision, and Sheffield United knocked it straight back, resulting in the second offside. But because it had been knocked back so quickly, they hadn't time to stop the game for the first decision, and so both linesmen had their flags up for offside.

So apart from the great tradition of midfield play, the art of defending was dying in England too, with everyone playing offside and then banging the free kick down to the other end of the park. Not that the players themselves were all bad. Towards the end of the 1980s, Leeds had Gordon Strachan, a top-class player, one of the best I've seen on the right of midfield. He was joined by Gary McAllister, another real footballer, an old-fashioned inside-forward, a schemer. There weren't many like him, and in fact there are not many like him today. He and Strachan and Gary Speed complemented each other. Speed was good, very brave, a really excellent header of the ball.

Arsenal had better players all round than Wimbledon, such as Paul Merson and Tony Adams, but they were playing the same sort of football in a slightly more sophisticated way. There was the added danger of the copycat effect. Because you didn't really need to know anything about the game to play it the POMO way, it was easy to copy. It would not be so easy to copy the way that, say, Barcelona have been playing in recent times. But if you wanted to do as well as Watford were doing, all you needed were the two big fellows up front, the two big fellows at the back, and a goalkeeper who could kick it the length of the pitch, and you were nearly there.

Good players, playing the game the right way, will always expose these guys. And if they are as good as Diego Maradona, who in 1986 famously exposed even the best English players of that period, it causes a shock to the system that is felt for a very long time. It is probably not entirely a coincidence that during these bleak years in English football, the national team was not doing very well either. The situation was not improved by the ban on English teams playing in European competitions after the 1985 Heysel Stadium disaster – the disease of hooliganism was dragging the English game through the dirt. Even Liverpool, for all the success they had had playing football as it should be played, had been caught up in the ugliness. Partly because of the behaviour of their own fans at Heysel, the club that won a fourth European Cup in 1984 was now isolated from the rest of the continent.

With this increasing sense of England as the sick man of football in every way, the other major nations were still trying to stick to their traditional principles. If anything, at the 1982 World Cup in Spain, the Brazilians were overdoing it. They had these typically brilliant players like Zico, Socrates and Falcao but, as I watched them in that tournament I could sense an important difference between this team and the great team of 1970. I felt that they had got too involved with the publicity surrounding them, which is something that can happen at a World Cup, and which showed itself not so much in the performances of their outstanding players, but in the approach of a player such as Junior, the left-back. He was getting a lot of publicity for the entertaining way in which he was playing, but basically a defender is a defender. It is his job to feed the ball to the people in front of him, to give it to the people who can play. And it must be that way, no matter how good the defender is – even a Beckenbauer or a Bobby Moore must give it to someone else, in order to get back and defend.

Occasionally, it is true, you have to dribble it forward, and you have to know when that is appropriate. But the reason why you should avoid that most of the time is simple – if you run past your own midfield player instead of giving it to him, and you lose the ball, the two of you are out of the game and the team is now obviously exposed at the back. If a midfielder loses it, you are still goalside to retrieve the situation. So a defender has to be humble. If I am a defender, I get it and I give it. In that Brazil team, the left-back Junior would get it, and instead of giving it to a colleague in front of him, he dribbled with the ball, trying to put on a show. Whether it is Brazil or any other team, that is wrong. Junior's play was a sure sign that they weren't as well managed as they should have been, and indeed I later read that the manager Tele Santana wanted the players to put on a show, so he had actually encouraged this bad play. Which created this impresssion that half the team – Zico, Socrates, Falcao and Junior – were involved in this contest to be the next Pelé, the next Jairzinho, the next Gerson or Tostão.

The manager should have been telling the full-backs, 'I don't care how good you are on the ball, if Socrates or Zico are in front of you, you give it to them.' But it seems that if anything, the manager was saying the opposite, telling them to fire away and to entertain the crowd. Brazil in 1982 didn't fully understand that Pelé was a team player, that all those great players of 1970 had been team players, doing it for one another. So the 1982 team was inspired by the 1970 team, but not necessarily in the right way. They had the individual talent to win the World Cup, but they were beaten by Italy, who played like a team – Italy who were also inspired by their own traditions, but in the right way.

Italy has produced so many absolutely brilliant players over the years, and here they were again with the likes of Bruno Conti, who reached greatness in that tournament. He was brilliant on the ball, industrious, a little bit like David Silva but with more 'go' in him. Conti could make goals and score goals, a really impressive player. There was Marco Tardelli who was a real goer, one of those all-action players, and there was the classic finisher Paolo Rossi. And though they all had those Italian virtues of excellent technique, they could also produce it under pressure, not for themselves but for the greater good, guided by the manager Enzo Bearzot – you would not hear Bearzot saying that football was all about putting on a show.

The West Germany side that they beat in the final would have all those good habits too, the right attitude and good organisation. But these were not great years for Germany. They were by no means as bad as the years that England were enduring, but their coaching philosophy had changed too, and not for the better. They were now more stereotypical. They didn't play with the freedom of the 1970s teams, an observation that might surprise some readers who feel that Germany have always played in roughly the same way. But in fact there was more fluency in the great teams of Beckenbauer and Overath and Müller, and those players just had a bit more class than the ones who came after them.

There was Karl-Heinz Rummenigge, a very good player but

maybe just a bit below the highest standards set during the Beckenbauer era. Or maybe it was just because he was playing in a less talented team. Then there was Lothar Matthäus, a typical West German player of the 1980s, fit and very effective as the best German players had always been, but not quite in the same class as a Günter Netzer. Their decline was gradual – it can take a while to go downhill – but it wasn't really until recent times that Germany started producing players of variety again. Nor were they exactly the most loved team of 1982, or of the decade in general, after the notorious scene in the World Cup semi-final in which the goalkeeper Schumacher 'took out' Patrick Battiston of France.

That French team had plenty of fluency and variety, because they were reaping the rewards of a more enlightened youth policy, a reconstruction that had begun around the mid-1970s. These progressive moves had also been taking place in countries such as Denmark which was producing players of the calibre of Michael Laudrup, technically good, an outstanding player all round, perhaps not quite up there with the true greats, though that is not to take anything away from him.

I played against most of the French over those years – Marius Trésor, Alain Giresse, Dominique Rocheteau and our old friend Michel Platini, who would lead them to triumph on home soil in the 1984 European Championship, despite the best efforts of the RTÉ panel at the time to explain that though Platini was very good in many ways, he should not be ranked among the game's immortals. In his club football, Platini formed a devastating partnership at Juventus with the Polish star Zbigniew Boniek, an out-and-out striker who was lightning quick, and who scored a lot of goals thanks mainly to Platini's excellent delivery of the ball.

England, who had not seen the need for reconstruction of the French kind, or of any kind, were just not up there any more. But there was Bryan Robson, a terrific player who was a young lad at West Bromwich Albion when I was there. I always found Bryan to be a good trainer, with a good attitude, and he soon established himself as a midfield payer with West Brom, then Manchester United and England. But I actually think that his best position would have been in the middle of the back four, like Bobby Moore. I think he could have played that role in his sleep, because Bryan wasn't particularly quick, but he could read it well. It was just that he was too valuable a player in midfield to be given a defensive role. He played left-back for me at West Brom, but Bryan could play in most positions. He was one of the best trackers in the game – when the opposing midfield player is on the ball, to track him is to get after him, get a tackle in, win the ball back. Bryan was also a very good header of the ball, and very brave when attacking the ball in the air in general. He scored a lot of valuable goals that way. England would never be entirely out of it, as long as they had players like Bryan Robson. And they managed to qualify for the 1986 World Cup in Mexico. There, they ran into Maradona.

For once, it was through no fault of their own that England had a bad day at a major tournament. Against any opposition at that time, and for some time to come, Maradona was a wonder of a player. You get a lot of bullshit in football, and so you can still hear people complaining about the Maradona handball that led to the first Argentina goal, calling him a cheat. No one who loves this game would concern themselves with that, given the other goal scored by Maradona in that game, a goal that can only be described as absolute magic. As he ran more than half the field through most of the England team, beating Peter Beardsley, Peter Reid, Steve Hodge, Terry Fenwick, Terry Butcher and finally Peter Shilton, he was a vision of perfect control, pace and balance – and then the finish, everything wrapped up there. It was a run that only a genius like him could do. And the fact that he thought he could do it in the first place was itself a mark of genius.

That is why he is up there with the greats of the game. Johan Cruyff probably wasn't as good a dribbler as Maradona. You would not see Pelé himself beating as many players as Maradona did on that day, but then they all have their own special characteristics. Eusebio scored a lot of goals and was a terrific player all round, but he could not dribble like Maradona, and he was probably just behind Cruyff and Pelé anyway. He couldn't do it on his own, but Maradona could. Of all the great players, probably Maradona and Lionel Messi are the most alike. Like Messi, Maradona could beat a player at close quarters, he was quick as lightning, with great balance, and he could get his shot away. Like all the great players, he had a great football brain, knowing when to deliver a pass, when to hold on to it. I have played with guys who could beat anyone, but then couldn't get rid of the ball – they were brilliant dribblers, but they had no end product. When they had beaten their opponent, they wouldn't know where they were.

Maradona was still only in his mid-twenties in 1986, but I could see how good he was as early as 1979, when I played against him at Lansdowne Road in my last game for the Republic. Maradona came on at half-time in a scoreless draw – he hit the crossbar, and he was brilliant. You could tell that he was tremendously gifted. You could also see that Maradona was actually shorter than me, which is encouraging in itself and further proof that this game is not all about the brute force of Wimbledon. And despite the many controversies in which Maradona has been involved, he could not have done all that he did without being a good pro as well.

In Argentinian football in general, there had been terrible problems with discipline. It wasn't until the World Cup of 1978, held in Argentina itself, that the manager César Luis Menotti got a grip of them and said that unless they get their discipline right, they would win nothing. For that tournament, they had outstanding players such as Daniel Passarella at centre-half, the striker Mario Kempes and Ossie Ardiles in midfield, but this time, helped by the values instilled in them by Menotti, they did not throw it away. Maradona was already displaying all the signs of genius as a teenager, but he was considered just too young for that World Cup. As he grew in stature, he was increasingly kicked from start to finish by opponents who could think of no other way of stopping him, and yet despite his reputation as a temperamental lad, he managed to control himself enough to get his country to two World Cup finals, winning the one in Mexico. In the days when the players and especially the stars of Argentina were less disciplined, it would all have ended in chaos.

And when I say that he got his country to those two finals, I mean that he really did do most of it on his own. Obviously he had good players around him, but he was still carrying them in a way that Pelé did not have to carry the rest of the Brazil team of 1970. People can hardly recall the names of most of the players that Maradona had around him, but we clearly remember Jairzinho, Rivelino, Gerson, Tostão and Carlos Alberto. Some of us even remember Everaldo and Clodoaldo, but as for the Argentinians, we are hard pressed to go beyond Burruchaga and Valdano. Again they were not bad players by any means, but it is still clear that Maradona had more to do than Pelé, which gives us a better sense of the enormity of his achievement.

From the mid-1980s, he played his club football for Napoli, carrying them in 1986–1987 to their first Serie A title, as well as the Coppa Italia in 1987, the UEFA Cup in 1989 and another Serie A title in 1989–1990. He was also the leading goal scorer in Serie A in 1987–1988. This was at a time when Italian football was attracting the best players in the world, as they followed the money in the same way as they have tended to do from the 1950s. Again, while he was becoming increasingly caught up in ugly matters off the field, he was still performing at the highest professional level despite all the kicking. Years later, I was speaking to Ossie Ardiles, who was an RTÉ panellist during the 2010 World Cup, and he told me that Maradona was not just a wonderful player, he was also liked and respected by the other lads. Sure enough, you would not see Maradona having a go at inferior players, he would just get on with it.

When Ardiles had his testimonial at Spurs, just before the

1986 World Cup, Maradona came over to play in it, though he could have made all sorts of legitimate excuses not to be there. According to Ardiles, this was characteristic of the man who for all his individual problems still had the affection of his team-mates. Maradona would have respected Ardiles too, for what he achieved for Argentina in 1978. In his popularity with his fellow pros, he was not unlike George Best. I know from talking to Nobby Stiles that the Manchester United lads all liked George. They regarded the other stuff around him as just bullshit. As it did to George, the bullshit brought down Maradona in the end, but not before he had won many of the major honours of the game for teams that couldn't possibly have won them without him. He did not just make a difference, he made all the difference.

In that Italian league of the late 1980s, Maradona came across players of the cailbre of Ruud Gullit, Marco van Basten and Paolo Maldini. And that was just at AC Milan, where they were getting the reward for playing football, rather than that strange and brutal game that was being played in England, in which a generation of midfield players had been lost. Indeed before the Dutch players arrived at AC Milan, Ray Wilkins had been there for a couple of seasons. Ray was a very, very good passer of the ball, with good vision, but he needed time and space in which to use the abilities that he had. And because he didn't have a turn of pace, in a tight game he couldn't create that time and space. He lacked a bit of 'devil'. Ray was a good footballer, who played eighty-four times for England, but he would not be a part of this new Milan side managed by Arrigo Sacchi that became the top team in Europe. And though they are generally regarded as a team consisting mainly of the three Dutch players, Gullit, van Basten and Frank Rijkaard, in truth Milan already had great players in Paolo Maldini and Franco Baresi.

When it was all put together, they could not be stopped. Marco van Basten was up there with the very best who have played the game, and it was a tragedy for him and for the game that he had to retire because of a recurring ankle injury at a relatively young age. This guy could control the ball, he could lead the line, he could score spectacular goals – a really, really big player. And he would probably have gone on to gain an even bigger reputation if he had played long enough. He was elegant, had a great temperament and was a brilliant finisher. And he was now doing this in Italy, where the hardest place to play is up front.

The Italians are excellent defenders, who mark well, never giving you an inch. Eamon Dunphy speaks of a special gene that the Italians have that makes them love defending, taking as much pleasure in the art of stopping an opponent from scoring as the striker does from getting a goal. Baresi and Maldini, and later Fabio Cannavaro, would have been among the greatest exponents of that art. Oddly enough, they allowed midfield players a bit more room than they allowed the forwards. Indeed when Liam Brady was leaving Arsenal, he was leaning towards a move to Germany rather than Italy, because he thought that he would have a bit more space there in which to play. We spoke about it, and I told him that he'd be all right in Italy because, in my experience, the Italians didn't get as tight on the midfield players as they did in England. It seemed to be part of their culture to give more room in that area of the pitch, to concentrate on defending at the back.

Which means that to score goals in Italy, you have to be good. And Marco van Basten was top notch. I always thought Ruud Gullit was something of a free spirit. He didn't actually play up front, you had to give him a free role. Probably his knowledge of the game wasn't good but he had loads of talent. He was a big fellow, quick, with good control and heading ability, a good shot. What he lacked in knowledge, he made up for with his athleticism, making him world class. The reputations of Gullit and van Basten probably rubbed off to some extent on Frank Rijkaard, who was a good player for AC Milan and the Netherlands, very solid, but not really in the same class as the other two.

Certainly along with their Italian colleagues they were the shining lights of this period leading up to the 1990 World Cup, which appropriately enough was held in Italy.

It has to be said, too, that on the evidence of the quality of football played at Italia '90, the English way seemed to have spread into other areas of international football. The Republic, of course, reached the quarter-final without actually winning a game, their two goals set up by long kick-outs from Packie Bonner. The introduction of the back-pass rule would soon force the Republic, and everyone else, to consider more creative methods of play. And yet such was the achievement of that team, and of Big Jack in popularising the game in Ireland, that it was possible to forgive almost anything, except perhaps the scoreless draw against Egypt. Nor was it possible to forgive the poor football from many of the more seasoned nations, who seemed to be saving all their best energies for the penalty shootouts. So it is hardly surprising that one of the most popular images of that tournament was more of an emotional than a football moment. This was the weeping of Paul Gascoigne in the semi-final when he received the yellow card that would have put him out of the final.

Not that he ever had to cross that bridge, because of another penalty shootout. It was particularly sad that Stuart Pearce missed one of the penalties, because Pearce was a real player. I feel that the 'Psycho' label has taken something away from him, making him a cartoon figure when in fact he was much better than that. Pearce was a real driving force as captain of Nottingham Forest and for England. From the position of full-back, he took responsibility. He was aggressive, with a great attitude, and he could play. I think I would put Stuart Pearce in an all-time England team, certainly in my time.

For a while, he and Gazza and England at Italia '90 revived the football spirits of their country – while the tournament was not easy on the eye in football terms, it was greatly enjoyed on very other level in England as much as in the Republic, and in Gazza it seemed as if England at last had another great player. Of course it was not to be.

The case of Gazza is a human tragedy. He had the blessings of a great player. He was strong, with good dribbling ability, control and vision, all the qualities which could have put him up there with the best of them. But the angels who bring these gifts forgot to give him one thing – a good head, the mentality that must go along with the ability he had been given. You have to have that, in your personal as well as your professional life. Because the higher you get in the game, the greater the pressure. At that stage, you need to have a strong mind.

Not that Gazza was a bad lad at all. As far as I can gather from those who knew him, he was a very genuine individual, and the other lads liked him. Of course he was a character, and in the ranks of the great players, you don't find many of them. Things might have worked out differently for him if he'd gone to Liverpool or Manchester United, rather than Tottenham, but I'm not so sure. Sir Alex Ferguson feels that if he'd got his hands on Gazza at the right time, Gazza might have been spared a lot of grief – or at least the wrong sort of grief. Ferguson could justifiably point to the way that he had nurtured Ryan Giggs and the other young lads at United as evidence of his ability to keep a precocious young player on the right road.

But again I doubt it. I feel that Gazza was always going to go the way he did, that he was always going to be attracted to London and all the showbusiness stuff that went along with it. I think that he did love the game, but he was the sort of lad who wants to please everyone and ends up pleasing no one, not even himself. I remember seeing him at an event in London where he was being presented with a prize by Jack Charlton. They were on this little stage, and when Jack gave him the prize, Gazza said, 'Thanks very much, Bobby.'

Everyone laughed at his 'mistake', but it was a contrived mistake. Gazza was a natural actor.

When I met him myself at an awards ceremony, not long after Italia '90, I found him friendly and even respectful, though there was a somewhat sad end to the evening. It had started off in good spirits with a presentation to the Best 100 Players in the Football League, an event organised with the backing of the FA, featuring players from the present day, all the way back to Tom Finney himself.

Finney was there, and as we all lined up in alphabetical order for the presentation, I was stood next to Gazza and Finney was not that far away from us. But in actuality, the distance between Tom Finney and Paul Gascoigne was vast. Finney was still a very modest, quiet man, who had never been involved in any controversy in his life. To him, Gazza would be like the man from Mars. But Gazza and I were side by side, and we fell into conversation, just having a laugh really.

'Are you off the jar?' I said to him.

'I just have the occasional glass of wine, you know?' he replied.

We both found it funny, but I knew there was more to it than that. I have some knowledge of alcoholism in general because a close friend, who has been in recovery for a long time, has been through it, and over the years has made me aware of how it works. So while a lot of people might have listened to Gazza talking about his occasional glass of wine and thought that he's doing pretty well to be drinking so little, I knew that this didn't sound right at all. If you've got a drink problem, as Gazza undoubtedly did, and you are still drinking to any extent – yes, even the occasional glass of wine – you are still in a lot of trouble. I knew from what my friend had told me that there isn't much of a halfway house there.

I said it to Gazza. 'Well, you're not off it then, are you?'

The tone of the conversation was still light. He just grinned, and we didn't take it any further. But later on, with the night almost finished, I was in a corridor in the hotel when the lift door opened and there was Gazza, now accompanied by a load of hangers-on, clearly very drunk. He recognised me, and he gave me a big hello. He said they were all going upstairs for a drink, and asked me if I wanted to come.

This was the guy who had the occasional glass of wine. I left them to it. I just felt sad for Gazza, a good lad in many ways, with the most awful problems.

11

Fergie

Of the many mind-boggling facts and figures you can cite about Alex Ferguson, one of the more striking is that, at the time of Italia '90, he had been manager of Manchester United for nearly four years. He was there when Gazza was at his peak – which seems like a long time ago, probably because it is a long time ago. The Premier League had not started when Ferguson was having his first major crisis, which he overcame, of course. In fact, everything about Ferguson is so singular, that he seems to be only vaguely connected to the job of management as it is practised by other men. When management in general is being discussed, there are many popular theories – you often hear it said that great players don't necessarily make great managers. That the best managers tend to be players who had mediocre careers, because they are still unsatisfied by what they have achieved in the game, and this gives them the drive to succeed in management. According to this theory, it also means that they can relate to the problems of the players that they manage, their weaknesses and insecurities, because they have encountered such problems themselves. In this analysis, the great players are already fulfilled by all that they have done in the game, and eventually they just get bored by the dreary business of trying to explain to inferior players things that came naturally to them.

Like a lot of popular theories about the game, it has some truth to it, but unfortunately it's not quite right. It approaches the matter in the wrong way. For a start, there are not that many great players out there, by comparison with the lesser variety. And there aren't that many great managers out there either – of any kind. If there was any reliable guide to picking a manager, based on any criteria, the game of football would be a lot easier for everyone. Unfortunately football is not like that, it is not simple. It just looks that way to some people, but in fact it is very, very complex. And because some 'experts' know a little about it, they think they know a lot. They don't realise how much they don't know.

So they will have these ideas about what makes a great manager when they should be a lot more humble about it and put it like this – it's a guessing game. Managers who are successful over a long period are so few and far between, I would hate to have a lot of money riding on whether I could choose the right one. Always we must remember that football is a game of chance, that the best managers are the ones who can reduce that level of chance better than the rest. And all I know for sure is that the great ones should be cherished. In the modern era, Sir Alex Ferguson is clearly the greatest we have seen.

Management is a test, week by week, never mind month by month or year by year. And to do it so successfully for twenty-five years, as Ferguson has done, is incredible. We can marvel at it, but we can't fully compare it with the achievements of the great managers who came before him, for a few reasons. In any era, it seems that no two of these managers are alike. And as we have seen, a Revie or a Busby or a Shankly would have found it impossible to build their teams in today's environment where the players have the power. The creation of the Premier League has been one of the biggest changes in the history of the game, one that has further complicated the role of the manager. In fact, it has complicated everything, because since it was formed in 1992, it has become so powerful in so many ways, there are some who seem to believe that there was no football at all before it started. Sky Sports will tell you that Alan Shearer is the first player to score a hundred league goals for two different clubs, ignoring that fact that Jimmy Greaves did it about fifty years ago.

The Premier League was set up for one reason and one reason only – to make more money for the leading clubs. And because it got so big, it is too big now for a manager to run a club in the way that he would like to run it. You've got chief executives now, directors of football, all sorts of functionaries diluting the power of the manager or even undermining him. Back in the 1940s, the club secretary was the most important man at every club. And it was only after a long fight over the years that the managers became more independent – or so it seemed. Even Shankly, who certainly gave all the appearance of being the most important man at Liverpool, still had his struggles. I recall that Johnny Morrissey was sold to Everton by the club rather than the manager.

Now with all these new layers of executives, if anything, the modern manager is in a slightly worse situation than his counterparts in the 1940s, who only had one club secretary to deal with. Probably the most important part of any manager's job is the signing of players, and yet it is now quite common for this to be done by the director of football, with the manager merely coaching the players that somebody else brings to the club. This may work if the director of football is himself chosen by the manager – at Manchester United, one of the chief scouts is Alex Ferguson's brother – but in some cases you'll find the director of football, or some such individual with executive powers, actively going against the manager's wishes, signing only the players that he wants, spinning stories to the manager that a deal couldn't be done because they couldn't agree terms with the player's agent or because the player's wife wants to live somewhere else or whatever.

It is tougher for managers at the lower levels too. With so much of the Sky money concentrated at the top, it is hardly worthwhile for a club in the lower leagues to have a youth policy. Transfer fees and a better distribution of wealth in general could ensure a higher standard overall. These days it would not be possible for a Brian Clough to do the spectacular things that he did with a club like Derby County or Nottingham

Forest – unless of course some sheikh pumped a few billion into it.

There may be huge money in the game, but there is still an equally huge reluctance on the part of the men with the money to trust someone else with that money – and certainly not to trust one person, the manager. It has always been like that, it's just that there's a lot more money now. I think of a man such as Bob Paisley who was like one of those little fellows with a flat cap who works with horses, and who is able to tell you whether or not to spend £4 million on a yearling, but otherwise is not really able to express himself at all. You can imagine the money-men of football today being presented with an unworldly character like Paisley, and thinking, 'Why the hell are we listening to this guy?'

If they were in any other business, these rich men would look at the most successful model out there, and they would try to copy that. In football, that would be Manchester United, where the manager is still the most important person at the club, because Alex Ferguson has won an almost unique level of control for himself over the years. But the owners just can't bring themselves to do that. And in the case of Roman Abramovich, not only does he not give the manager the power that he needs, he just goes out and buys players that he likes himself, regardless of what the manager thinks. Everything was going well at Chelsea for a few seasons with José Mourinho, who was in control of team matters for a while, until Abramovich started buying players like Shevchenko and Ballack. Obviously Mourinho knew that this couldn't work, at least not while he was still the manager. And as a result, Abramovich went through several other managers and countless millions trying to get what he already had with Mourinho.

At Liverpool, there was Rafael Benitez, who won the Champions League in 2005, and who still ran into a classic power struggle, looking for the sort of control that Ferguson had at United. He was also unfortunate in that Liverpool's American owners were not even of the same calibre as United's American owners, who have been fiercely criticised on many counts, all justified I am sure, but who have actually been quite good owners in the sense of letting Ferguson get on with it.

Arsène Wenger has been given the freedom to do a lot at Arsenal, but then to some extent Wenger went native, as they say, with the directors. The traditional struggle has always been between the manager wanting to spend money, and the directors resisting it. So if, like Wenger, you are telling the directors that actually you don't want to go out and buy players, that you want to develop your young players instead, it must be music to their ears. You won't hear the Arsenal directors saying a bad word about Wenger, though Arsenal haven't won anything for quite a while. They are happy with the state of the bank balance, whereas the supporters don't give a damn about the bank balance. They don't want to wait for some long-term policy to mature, for them it takes too long – even for Cesc Fabregas it took too long.

Of course Wenger has won things at Arsenal, culminating in the amazing unbeaten record in 2003–2004 of the team they called 'The Invincibles', and he is undoubtedly a great football man. But if you compare him with Ferguson, who is always replenishing the team with expensive new signings as well as by developing young talent, you can see why that gap has grown between the two clubs. Wenger then had to listen to Robin van Persie expressing his dissatisfaction at the direction in which the club was going, when it seemed that van Persie himself was only going in one direction – to where the big money was waiting for him, after his one unquestionably brilliant season with Arsenal.

Ferguson had to listen to something similar from Wayne Rooney, but Ferguson was in a stronger position. Not only has he constantly replenished, he continued to win things while he was replenishing. He knows that that requires money. Liverpool did it at their peak, astutely buying the best players available – Kenny Dalglish, Graeme Souness, John Barnes – to keep the success rolling along. They weren't prepared to wait until next year, hoping that the young players would come through. Ferguson too would be saying, 'I don't give a shit about next year.' He wants to win this league, this year.

He will have noted that as soon as Manchester City won the Premier League, even after the mind-boggling amounts of money that had already been spent, Roberto Mancini was complaining that the sporting director Brian Marwood wasn't spending more. Ferguson will know exactly where Mancini is coming from. Ferguson has seen plenty of managers who went along with the directors, not demanding money, balancing the books, and who got sacked in the end. Because eventually it is the supporters who get the manager sacked, the supporters who, like Ferguson, don't give a shit about next year.

Along the way, Ferguson has bought well and he has bought badly. He signed Roy Keane and Eric Cantona, he also signed

Eric Djemba-Djemba and Bebe. But then there hasn't been a manager born who has been right all the time. Busby and Shankly bought a few bummers themselves. Towards the end of his first highly successful period as Liverpool manager, Kenny Dalglish signed a few who weren't really Liverpool players. Again there is a guessing game involved but the best managers are more right than they are wrong. And because the club is being run properly, if they make a mistake, they realise it, and they do something about it.

Alex Ferguson has been doing it for a long time, to a miraculous extent, and he has been doing it without even showing a great knowledge of the technical aspects of the game. Then again, I don't think Bill Shankly had that either. And I know that Brian Clough didn't. I remember when Clough was at Leeds United and we came in at half-time having lost two goals from corner kicks against Aston Villa, Norman Hunter said to Clough, 'We don't know who we're supposed to be picking up.'

'You're an England international,' Clough replied. 'You sort it out when you get out there.'

Don Revie, by contrast, was brilliant at the technical aspects, but he wouldn't have the bigger picture that Clough had. None of the great managers has been perfect. If we suppose that there are five aspects to management, the ones who have four of them are doing very well. You could see an example of a fault in Ferguson when David Beckham was playing on the right side of midfield. He would be too far ahead of the ball. He could have been in a deeper or a wider position to receive the ball. And the full-backs could have been in better covering positions.

Again, Don Revie wouldn't have allowed that to happen, partly because he didn't start out with the luxury of having top players at his disposal, so he had to work very hard with them on their positioning, their defending, how they could correct mistakes and improve from match to match. With such a well-drilled team, you start to develop a consistency, and you start to concede fewer goals.

Ferguson would not see the fine detail of the mistakes that Don would have seen, and put right. But Ferguson has a natural optimism, which Don did not have. He fully expects every team that he puts out there to win. In fact I don't think I've ever seen anyone with such optimism, and as an asset in management you can't overstate it. Certainly it makes up for whatever he lacks in knowledge, and maybe a man of his temperament is better off not knowing too much on the technical side. It's a bit like the guy who gets on a plane – if you know how the plane works, maybe you'll never get on it in the first place. But with that huge confidence which he has in his players, Ferguson will put out a side against Arsenal in the quarter-final of the FA Cup that has Anderson and Silva in midfield alongside Ireland's Darron Gibson and John O'Shea, a bizarre and an apparently hopeless proposition against an Arsenal side managed by a man of Arsène Wenger's deep knowledge and insight. With Ferguson the glass is not half-full or half-empty, it is always overflowing – 'Darron Gibson and John O'Shea are going to do it,' he believes – and they did. United won that match by two goals to nil.

It may also explain his bad behaviour when he loses. Another manager might be trying to analyse why he lost, but Ferguson wouldn't have that instinct for the technical side.

With that total absence of doubt in his mind, he simply can't understand why his team lost, so he just blows up.

Not that he is stupidly optimistic. When he had to get rid of players like Jaap Stam – or even Roy Keane – he got rid of them. There is that ruthlessness to do whatever is right for the club, a total lack of sentimentality. But then if he was an overly sensitive type of fellow, Ferguson probably would not have survived. To have been in management so long, there has to be something lacking at a human level – even as he passed the age of seventy, it was as important to him as it always has been.

He doesn't see irony, for example, or even hypocisy. The TV cameras caught Wayne Rooney elbowing James McCarthy of Wigan, an offence for which Rooney should have been sent off. Then Manchester United are playing Chelsea and David Luiz commits a cynical foul, with Ferguson rightly claiming that Luiz should have been sent off. And yet Rooney, who scored against Chelsea, shouldn't have been on the pitch in the first place – he should have been serving the suspension for the red card he should have got for fouling McCarthy. Ferguson has a long memory or no memory, depending on what suits him.

But then during my own playing days, I was aware of a sort of tunnel vision in myself. In fact I have seen it so often, and seen how it can work to your advantage, it has led me to this conclusion – in football, and football management in particular, you don't want to be too well-rounded.

And then, for no reason that we can fathom except that he is a genius, Ferguson can confound his own reputation for tunnel vision in the most surprising ways. In relation to Eric Cantona and Cristiano Ronaldo, for example, there is no doubt that Ferguson's management was extraordinary. Indeed he probably deserves more credit for what he did with Ronaldo and Cantona than he actually gets. And they, in turn, should probably get less credit. Personally I wouldn't have had them at all. I couldn't have indulged them the way Ferguson did, and I wouldn't be alone in that. I'm sure, for example, that Don Revie, or indeed Bill Shankly or Jock Stein, wouldn't have indulged them either.

But Ferguson, by being pragmatic, by applying different criteria to them than he did to others, managed to get the best out of them, with the result that they became really important players for Manchester United – at least at certain times. Cantona never really did it for United in Europe, just as he had never done it at international level, playing no part whatsoever in France's great run of success in the late 1990s. In fact he hadn't done much at Leeds United either, or any other team, before he was signed by Ferguson, who somehow saw this quality in him that others either hadn't seen or hadn't been able to nurture. By doing that, Ferguson demonstrated his own greatness, his willingness to suppress many of his own basic instincts about the game in order to achieve what he felt was the greater good. He showed that he could endure these horrible frustrations, up to and including the night when he had to watch Cantona aiming a spectacular kung-fu kick at a spectator at Selhurst Park for reasons that could only be imagined.

It was really fascinating to see how he made something

work at United, at a particular time, in a particular way, that couldn't be repeated in any other situation. He realised back then that United needed a hero, because they'd blown the league the previous season, allowing Leeds United to win it. And he felt that Eric Cantona would be the man for the job. And Cantona didn't need any persuading, casting himself in that role without a second thought, realising that at last he had found a stage that was worthy of him, one on which he could finally perform – but not in the Champions League. He scored a late winner in the FA Cup final against Liverpool, something for which that match is mainly remembered, yet it was Roy Keane, not Cantona, who had been brilliant in that game for United. So, yes, he was a great signing, perhaps one of the greatest signings in the history of the game, but I couldn't put it stronger than that.

Ronaldo, by contrast, was able to do it at the highest level, up to and including the final of the Champions League – at least the one against Chelsea, not the one against Barcelona – but only if he was permitted by Ferguson to remonstrate with his colleagues on the pitch, to feign injury and to ignore the defensive side of the game, factors which should be noted by anyone putting him up there with Messi.

I believe that Ferguson has a reverence for the great players, and that, above all, he would love to have been a great player himself. As such he would probably come under that broad category of men who didn't make it to the top during their playing days, and who, as a result, are driven to succeed as managers. But really, Ferguson has put himself beyond all categories.

What we can say is that his appreciation of the great players has helped him to bring the right players to Manchester United, and to give a chance to the kids who were there already, to Scholes, Giggs, Beckham, Butt and the Nevilles. It was a remarkable decision, to bring those young players into what was already a winning team, not just defying all who doubted him at the time, but forming the backbone of the team for many years to come. And he has always trusted his players to perform, to play good football, to believe in themselves as he believes in them.

Ferguson would have absolutely loved the great Scottish players such as Denis Law, he would have idolised Jim Baxter. To have been one of those great Scottish players himself would have been the ultimate achievement for him, which may throw some interesting light on his relationship over the years with probably the greatest Scottish player of them all, Kenny Dalglish.

With almost everyone else in football, Ferguson would feel that he has a natural advantage. We can see how other managers in the Premier League defer to him, the way that he dominates them. He knows that he has their number. But with Dalglish he knows that, if anything, it is the other way round. They both know it. Dalglish is that thing that Fergie always wanted to be, a great Scottish player and, as such, Dalglish has never been intimidated by what Ferguson has achieved, as so many others in the game have been.

Most of the other managers in England have only come across Ferguson as a manager. But Kenny was a wonder boy who was just starting his career at Celtic when Ferguson was finishing his at Rangers, and for Fergie to have become such a huge figure in the game later on must have seemed to Kenny a bit like one of those movies in which the kid who grew up next door to you and who seemed like nothing special goes on to become a big star.

No matter how many honours he has won at United, I suspect that somewhere deep down Ferguson would always feel that Dalglish has this natural superiority that comes from being an aristocrat of the game, a great player, up there with Denis Law and Jimmy Johnstone.

I played against Fergie, drawing with Rangers at Ibrox and beating them 2–0 at Elland Road. He was an honest centre-forward, who scored a fair number of goals for Rangers, but he was not a Dalglish, a Law or a Baxter. In fact, he never played for Scotland.

But as a manager he has become one of the immortals. As Kenny Dalglish was leaving Liverpool at the end of the 2011–2012 season, having stabilised the club but having failed to put them back in contention for the Premier League, Ferguson at the age of seventy was still competing for the title until the last minute of the last day.

Incredible.

12

The Premier League — the Great and the Good

The men who have challenged Alex Ferguson and even beaten him at times – Arsène Wenger and José Mourinho – brought their own kind of greatness to the game in England. Wenger has a different philosophy altogether to Ferguson about the way the game should be played. But he proved that his philosophy is a winning one too. Recently, he has found it more difficult to replenish his team, but at the start he had the advantage that managers can sometimes have in the early days – he knew about players who were available that no one else recognised at the time, or at least that they hadn't evaluated properly – in Wenger's case, the French players such as Patrick Vieira, Emmanuel Petit, Nicolas Anelka and Thierry Henry.

I remember something similar, but on a smaller scale, when I started out as player-manager of West Bromwich Albion in the mid-1970s, because I knew about Irish players who were generally underrated in the English game. Once Wenger had brought in the right players at the start, for a long time he didn't have to replenish, because he was able to convey his ideas to the players who were already there, encouraging Tony Adams, Martin Keown, Lee Dixon and Nigel Winterburn to express themselves more than they had done with George Graham. And also encouraging the French players to make it easy for them.

Before Wenger arrived, no one would have believed that Tony Adams could come out and play. And yet Adams was not being asked to do too much, because Wenger had organised things in such away that Adams would have someone to pass the ball to, ten yards away. We know that Wenger would eventually find it difficult to keep bringing in players of the calibre of Vieira, and developing players of the stature of Adams, relying instead on a youth policy which has ultimately failed. Yet he undoubtedly brought something brilliant to the Premier League that hadn't been there before.

José Mourinho actually dominated Ferguson for a while, which is a mark of greatness in itself, leaving aside all the other things he has won in Portugal, Italy and Spain. I thought he was terrific, winning the league in his first season, coming into Chelsea where there was a perception of these huge egos who were difficult to manage. Mourinho obviously has the ability to form good relationships with the people who matter most, the players. His biggest problem is his insecurity, the way he pursues a certain type of celebrity that has nothing to do with his coaching abilities. Some commentators say that he's taking the pressure off the players by attracting publicity to himself, but I think that is total nonsense. He has this urge to make himself bigger than the teams he has managed, and he doesn't need it. Managers become bigger than their teams because of results, and Mourinho already had that. I don't want to see him as a character, I want to see him as a football man. Alex Ferguson may indulge in his own strange antics, but unpleasant as they may be, he is usually trying to get an edge, maybe trying to bully journalists or to influence referees or whatever. Mourinho is just seeking attention.

But as a football man, I would always be on his side and admire what he does. When Mourinho goes to a club, he insists that he is in charge. He wouldn't put up with Abramovich's interference at Chelsea, and at Real Madrid it seems that he has also won a battle for control. In that most important way, he always sticks to his principles. Despite my mixed emotions about his time in England, and the stupid, and indeed cruel, things that diminish his achievements, the greatness of Mourinho is evident in the four league titles he has won in different countries and in winning the Champions League with two different teams.

There are so many elements to being a manager, and few have it all. Rafa Benitez was a good disciplinarian who controlled the players well. I don't think he ever embraced Steven Gerrard or Jamie Carragher as another manager would have done, but he understood that his job was to get the best out of the players no matter what. And I never saw a Liverpool team giving less than 100 per cent for him. He may have kept the players at arm's length, but he had his own ideas, he would not be moved, there was no room for debate about what he wanted. And these are great attributes. And yet I never felt there was a proper connection between the players on the pitch. His team seemed to play by numbers, the left-back was the left-back, and if you got the ball there, you did a specific thing. A team of Arsène Wenger's, by contrast, had more cohesion, they were all close to each other, they had a level of interplay that wasn't there at Liverpool.

Nor would I be sure of Benitez's judgement of a player, whereas I think that that was the main strength of Harry Redknapp. Harry had a more old-fashioned approach than most of the modern managers, and I found it interesting that the older Harry got, the more important those values seemed to become. Harry never went to a fashionable coaching school, but in many ways that was a good thing. Not only was he a good judge of a player, he had an idea of how they should play, and then he let them do it. Others were getting too technical, believing in systems and tactics, rather than pure playing abilties, and bringing the right players to the club, which is by far the most important thing. Harry might be accused of working the transfer system in his own unique style, and ultimately of lacking the ambition to really challenge for the big prizes – a legacy, I feel, of his upbringing at West Ham. Yet, you never saw too many duds playing for his teams, at Portsmouth or Spurs.

Always we are back to the players. And if we are talking about the players of the past twenty years in England, the only place to start is with Paul Scholes. What made him special, particularly in his early years, was his ability to contribute what he did in midfield, and also to score a lot of goals. That is what I found remarkable, and why I would put him up there with the greats. There have been very, very few players who could do that. Martin Peters was one of the first to score a lot of goals by arriving into the box from midfield, but Martin contributed very little in the middle. Scholes was a genuine midfield player and, as he got older, and when Roy Keane was no longer in the team, he played in the middle in the classical sense, and scored fewer goals. In that role, he was as good as Xavi or Pirlo, and he was winning everything with United, though it was a shame that the England teams he played for were not doing well – not least because under Sven-Goran Eriksson, at one time Scholes was playing on the left. Personally I think that's why he gave up playing for England. Considering what he could do in the middle, for a player like that to be on the right or on the left was ridiculous. So he never got the opportunity at international level to display the full range of his abilities, and to have his greatness acknowledged even more.

Perhaps in his late thirties, when he came back to play for United after having 'retired', there was a heightened awareness that Scholes was not just a great player but possibly the last of an endangered species – the creative English midfield player. At Arsenal, there is Jack Wilshere, who is just starting, but otherwise in that role we've been looking at the likes of Luka Modrić, David Silva, Xabi Alonso and Yohan Cabaye. For the

English lads, not to mention the Scottish and the Irish lads, it seems to be a lost art.

Yet even though he was still doing it so well at the age of thirty-seven, Scholes does not have the sort of personality that would make him a celebrity in these times. He was never a character, he doesn't do interviews. I recently heard someone saying that Mario Balotelli is a great player, though Balotelli would be the polar opposite to Scholes, who would not be found taking his jersey off after he scores, getting a yellow card which might cost his team the game later on, or generally messing about and acting the clown. Because of his understated style, Scholes is less well known in England today than Robbie Savage. I also heard Jamie Redknapp on Sky, saying that Scholes doesn't get the credit he deserves, to which you can only say, 'Well, you guys give him the credit then!' Like his colleague Denis Irwin, Scholes was just a brilliant player, who got on with the job and just played football.

The same could obviously not be said of David Beckham, given the scale of his commitments outside the game. But he was a very talented and a very valuable player. He was not a great carrier of the ball, a great dribbler who could beat the full-backs, but he was an outstanding distributor of the ball on his right side, a good crosser. And he was brilliant from dead-ball situations. I admired him too for the brilliance with which he turned his football career into a huge international business. I would rather be talking about him as a great player than the richest footballer ever produced in Britain, and yet that is an achievement in itself.

I think again of Sven-Goran Eriksson, and how he has

mastered the game of management without really being much good at it. Management is one of the toughest things out there, you really need to be a survivor, so there's a part of me which appreciates the way that Eriksson has beaten the system. In fact, Eriksson has not just survived, he has succeeded in, among other things, making a vast fortune out of managing England unsuccessfully. Meanwhile there was poor old Alf Ramsey winning the World Cup and finishing his days in a public ward, skint. I look at a manipulator like Eriksson, and a commercial genius like Beckham, and I think of all the good players I knew who don't have a bob.

It is a different world, a different game, and yet the principles remain the same. There is still much to admire. Ryan Giggs, for example, is probably as close as anyone can get to being a great player, without quite being a great player. Which might seem harsh. And certainly I have been challenged on this over the years, by people who hold Ryan Giggs in the highest regard for all his outstanding qualities. In fact, I would be one of those people too. There are so many good things about Ryan Giggs as a player that it seems wrong to bring in any sort of a negative note. And yet if we are trying to make a distinction between the true greats and those who are perhaps not quite at that level, we find no better example than Giggs.

No doubt there are some who would happily place him alongside Pelé, Beckenbauer, Maradona and Messi, but I don't think I could fully go along with that. I love his attitude to the game, I think he has been a terrific player for Manchester United, for whom he has scored a lot of important goals, and I wish there were more like him. I would place him ahead of a player like Rio Ferdinand, who looks very good on the ball but who is not really my type of defender. I don't think he does the nitty-gritty of defending as well as Jamie Carragher did, for example, during Carragher's best seasons for Liverpool. And certainly you don't see him getting in as many blocks and tackles as John Terry. Again, Terry may not be as good on the ball as Ferdinand, but as regards the basics of defending, I would prefer Terry. I would also prefer Nemanja Vidić.

Nor does Rio Ferdinand really convince me with his badge-kissing, the way he wants to be first on the player's back when a goal is scored, sending out the message, 'Look how much I care.' I would certainly believe that Gary Neville had all that passion, whereas Ferdinand always seemed to be too aware of how everything looks, too tuned in to the media – and that was before Twitter.

I don't think I am being old-fashioned when I say that players have no business being on Twitter, simply because it seems to result in nothing but trouble. Why would you want that? Is there not enough trouble out there without inviting more of it into your life with some silly remark? In football generally there are always so many things that need to go right, if you want to succeed. A million little things need to be working in your favour, just to give you a chance. So the notion that players would be sitting at home telling the world what is on their mind at any given moment is just not a good idea, and personally I wouldn't have it.

Again I would praise Giggs for not letting these outside influences interfere with the important stuff, doing it for United as he has done for so long. In fact, given all the adulation he received when he started as a teenager, I am amazed that he managed to avoid becoming a media star like Beckham. Maybe Giggs just didn't have Beckham's flair in that department, but then if he did, we probably wouldn't be discussing his career in this context – it would probably have been all over a long time ago.

But I would still have to say that for all Giggs has brought to United, there is something lacking in his concentration at vital moments, something casual about the way he delivers the final ball. And he has been doing it for so long at this stage that he is unlikely to fix the problem.

I remember I had to deal with this issue of concentration in the early part of my own career, because it is crucial. I would see the full-back coming on the overlap and occasionally I would intend to pass it to him, only to knock it out of play. I'd be baffled by my own mental laziness – how the hell did I do that? Experience taught me that there are moments in the game when everything is exaggerated, like when you get to the end line and it is vital that you deliver the right ball. Over time, in these situations, in my mind I would hear a click. Now … concentrate.

After all, there's no point beating a few players and getting into these positions if you can't deliver the final ball. There's no point knocking it out of play or hitting it straight to the keeper or blasting it over the bar like the old-fashioned 'brainless winger' – sometimes dribbling doesn't need a lot of concentration. Again, you must hear that click. Now … concentrate.

Most of the time, poorer players don't get into the positions that a player of Ryan Giggs' ability does. And yet when he is about to deliver the ball, it can seem that he is not giving it his full attention. You see it too in dead-ball situations, when that full attention is most needed. It's a bit like the golfer who walks up to an eighteen-inch putt and taps it in casually, not giving it the high level of concentration he would give to a twelve-foot putt. In fact, the nearer you get to the hole, the more you should concentrate.

So Giggs will be taking a free kick or a corner kick. He'll place the ball down with his left hand, and then he will turn his back to it. I think this shows a lack of concentration. You should make sure that you place the ball properly and you should never take your eye off it in such an important moment. Having got into this situation, it is not good enough to turn your back on it, to turn around and to throw your leg at it. Because at times his mind seems to be elsewhere, Giggs doesn't make the most of his technique.

In football, you always do what you can see. The great players, like Kenny Dalglish, for example, will get into a position where they can see their options – and then they hold it. The first touch will buy them time to hold it, and if they hold it long enough, everything opens up. It gives their colleagues a chance to take up a position, and then they can pick out the right ball. That is, the most dangerous ball.

You wouldn't see Kenny dribbling like Maradona, but his final ball was terrific. Unlike Giggs, his mind seemed always to react in the right way to the options that he had. In football, you always have loads of options, but the great players usually pick the right option because their mind is calm. First their technique is very good. Kenny Dalglish's technique meant that he had a clear head. His mind was not cluttered by questions – How am I going to control the ball? Am I going to control the ball at all? – and this gave him the time and the space that he needed. And then he had the presence of mind to use it properly.

'Kenny always knew what he was doing before he did it,' the pundits used to say. But it wasn't true. He just made it look that way.

Steven Gerrard has not scored as many goals for Liverpool as Kenny, yet I am sure that Kenny appreciates what a good goal scorer Gerrard has been. Which might seeem like an odd place to start with Steven Gerrard, but this is what I have always felt about him – he is a very, very good goal scorer, and that is his main value to the team.

In fact, the goal he scored away to Marseille in the Champions League – a first-time shot from the edge of the area that dipped under the crossbar – is one of the best goals I have ever seen. And his goals have not just been brilliantly taken, they have been vitally important. There would have been no Champions League final in Istanbul in 2005 if Gerrard hadn't blasted in that late winner in the group stage against Olympiakos – and his headed goal in the final started the famous comeback. There was also his last-minute equaliser against West Ham in the 2006 FA Cup final, a brilliant shot from outside the box into the bottom left-hand corner. In any circumstances, it was a great goal – in the dying seconds of the cup final, it was remarkable.

Gerrard is a highly talented lad and a hugely valuable player. And yet he is not the player that most commentators seem to think he is. For years, they have been talking about his 'favoured central midfield role', when he is really not that kind of player at all. Gerrard himself throughout his career clearly believed that that is his best position, which is part of the problem. And Rafael Benitez, who seemed rightly convinced that that was not Gerrard's true role, was heavily criticised for going against the player and his supporters in the media.

And yet you only have to think of a real midfield general, such as Andrea Pirlo, to realise that Gerrard just doesn't do what players of that ilk have always done. At the 2012 European Championship, we saw Pirlo giving a master class in the art of the creative midfielder, always in the right position to receive the ball, distributing it beautifully, always involved in the game, as if it was second nature to him. There is no such continuity in Gerrard's play. He is a man for the dramatic, match-winning moments, but he can be absent from a game for long periods, far too long for a player in that position. Where was Gerrard when Pirlo was dominating? He should have been able to do something about it. You will see him sending a long pass out to the wing, a very good pass that lands at the feet of the player it is meant for, but then you will see him trotting up the field in the general direction of the play, as if his attention has started to wander.

What he should do when he delivers that pass is immediately to think, 'What can I do next?' But, again, that sense of continuity that you will find in a great midfielder like Pirlo is just not there. And if that's not there, it is impossible to dictate the game from the middle of the field. Your contribution is spasmodic.

I think of my own Leeds team, which was a very well-balanced side, and I wonder where you would have played Gerrard in that side. Would he have taken the place of Billy Bremner or Peter Lorimer? I don't think so. You could play him in a free role, but then you'd have to leave out Allan Clarke. And personally, I wouldn't recommend that. I would say that Gerrard's partner in the national side, Frank Lampard, is another player who has been wrongly labelled over the years, and this perhaps helps to explain why he and Gerrard could not play together in midfield for England, why we heard so much about the need for the two of them to be 'accommodated'.

Lampard has been as outstanding for Chelsea as Gerrard has been for Liverpool but, like Gerrard, perhaps his most important contribution has been as a goal scorer. Again he has not been a midfielder in the orthodox sense, not a Pirlo or a Paul Scholes. He has been a terrific lad, one of Chelsea's most valuable players and, like Gerrard, he played a vital role in driving his team to win the Champions League, but if we are applying the toughest standards, we have to say that if someone is truly a great player, they don't have to be 'accommodated'.

It is not easy being the complete player, which is why there are so few of them, and why we should identify them, and celebrate them.

Henrik Larsson, who was a colleague of Giggs' at United for a short spell, was, I believe, a genuinely great player. I think he was a really intelligent player, a great athlete and he had the sort of temperament that is usually described as being 'typically Swedish'. He never seemed to be involved in any 'incidents', but had the mature intelligence to just get on with the game in the interest of the team and of his own play. With Larsson, there was no side show.

He played for Celtic in the Scottish Premier League, which is hardly the best league out there, but we must remember that Celtic also played in the Champions League every year, so Larsson played at the top level as much, if not more, than some of the leading players in England. He also scored a lot of goals for Sweden. And towards the end of his career, he won the Champions League with Barcelona, when they beat Arsenal 2–1 in the 2006 final. It is always interesting to see how a player is rated by his colleagues or his opponents and, in the case of Larsson, we have the words of Thierry Henry, who said it was not Ronaldinho or Samuel Eto'o who made the difference in that Champions League final, but Larsson who came on as a substitute and made both goals.

Henry himself reached greatness at Arsenal, of that there is no doubt. And yet it was for a limited period of time. Did he fufil his true potential? I don't think so. For a couple of years in Wenger's most outstanding side, he was certainly world class. But given what he had achieved, I was a bit disappointed at how quickly he went out of it. For a couple of seasons towards the end, he didn't really contribute at all, and at times he was actually poor. He didn't do it at Barcelona either. A lot of the great players were still great at the age of thirty-two or even thirty-four, but with Henry you got the sense that he had said to himself, 'I've done enough.'

There are some who would simply say that Henry was great, without qualification, but then is that not taking something away from a player such as Paolo Maldini? Here was a fantastic player, who was trying his best, improving all the time into his late thirties for AC Milan. The money, all the things that he had already won, didn't mean anything at that stage; for Maldini it was about the satisfaction of getting the most out of what he had.

Tony Adams would also have had that sense of satisfaction. He achieved a form of greatness because of his attitude and his ability to defend – and, under Wenger, that determination to keep improving. He may not have had Maldini's class, or that of Maldini's colleague at centre-half at AC Milan, Alessandro Nesta, but he had this great heart and a will to win. He was big, strong, a real leader when Arsenal were up against it, like Roy Keane was for United. I think he gave everything to Arsenal, and to England, though England were obviously not as well organised. Others might have appeared to give everything to their clubs, but Adams was the real thing.

Patrick Vieira came pretty close to it as well. He had a huge effect when he arrived, and at his best he would be up there with the leading players we have seen in the Premier League. I think that Roy Keane did more for United, over a longer period, but he was a diffrent type of player. Vieira had more skill and creativity than Keane, but I don't think he had the same drive. I don't think anyone had the same drive. But Vieira was one of the few who could play in a genuine midfield role in recent times. He could command the middle of the pitch, he could tackle and win the ball. Robert Pires, too, was a very, very good player and a good servant for Arsenal, as was Ashley Cole until he decided to take his talents to Chelsea. I wouldn't quite put Cole up there with Maldini, and I think that Denis Irwin was a more natural footballer – Cole is a little bit manufactured by comparison. But he has been effective and industrious, and he has done it when it mattered.

Dennis Bergkamp was definitely a natural footballer, a very talented lad, and yet I never saw him as a great player. He could always make a difference with his ability and his class, but I never thought there was any great urgency or passion about him, or that you could entirely depend on him. He tended to go with the flow. On his day, he could be absolutely brilliant, but whenever you find yourself saying 'on his day', you are probably not talking about a great player. Let us make special mention, too, of David Seaman, who was not only the best English goalkeeper of his generation, but the last top-class English keeper until the arrival of Joe Hart.

At Liverpool, they haven't been producing the great players for a long time, so it is no accident that they have been mostly out of contention for the big trophies for a while. John Barnes, whose career spanned the old First Division and the Premier League, was very close to being great. He played in Liverpool teams when they were winning things, and he was hugely influential because he could beat players with a piece of magic. I thought his positional sense was a bit suspect, certainly when compared with that of John Robertson. But for a while with Liverpool, Barnes was about three-quarters of the way up the mountain.

Peter Beardsley, who was one of the leading players for England, was a player I knew well, having bought him from Carlisle United when I was manager at Vancouver Whitecaps. Peter was quite a way up the mountain too. He was a very,

very valuable player, a Roy of the Rovers type. He would have several things in his head that he wanted to do with the ball. At Vancouver, I tried to get him to make Kenny Dalglish his role model. First, like Kenny, you must control it. Peter would want to do three different things but I tried to get him to do first things first. When eventually he went to Newcastle in the 1990s, I don't think he had ever quite lost the Roy of the Rovers tendencies, but he always had this trick, always a way of doing something different.

Robbie Fowler was a great finisher for a certain period. If he had continued to mature, and to improve on what he had, he could have been one of the true Liverpool immortals. But I got the impression that he didn't work at it, and he was further diminished by injuries. Michael Owen was also a could-have-been. When he started out, I certainly thought that he had the potential to break all the goal-scoring records going, with his pace, his finishing ability and his attitude, which was always good, but he had one injury after another and eventually his career started to drift. It shows us again how fragile it all can be with players, not just footballers but golfers or tennis players who need so many things to go right for them, just to stay fit, or else they end up in this place where they could-have-been or they might-have-been. Stan Collymore was a could-have-been of major proportions, one of the originals. Stan could play, he had a lot of ability, but he also had a lot of excuses. In the end, it was all just a waste.

Even Manchester United under Ferguson have had their could-have-beens, such as Dwight Yorke – though Yorke contributed far more to United than Collymore did to Liverpool. When I say that Yorke was a could-have-been, I mean that he really was very gifted, and I think he had the ability to be better than he was, for longer than he was. He had good control, good technique, he was quick and, for a certain period, he did it for United, up to and including their fabulous Treble in 1999. Yorke was a really valuable player. But he was one of those lads who did it for a relatively short time, and who seemed satisfied by what he had done. Maybe his lifestyle caught up with him but, for whatever reason, he didn't march on. In my own career, I have seen the amount of hard work, determination and application you need to keep going at the top for as long as it lasts. I think of a player like Nemanja Vidić, a terrific defender who was a real driving force for United, and definitely on his way to being a great player, coming on to his best years, when he was struck down by a cruciate ligament injury. The great players are pushing on at that age, doing everything it takes to reach the pinnacle of their careers. I hope that Vidić makes it there.

John Terry has probably attracted even more colourful publicity than the likes of Collymore and Yorke did in their day, but on the pitch he has been a different man altogether. I would put him in the same bracket as Tony Adams. Terry has the drive to do it, he is good in the air, a good tackler who puts his body on the line, all those qualities of the natural defender. He would fall short of Beckenbauer, who could do all those things but who had much more ability. And at international level, he wouldn't be a Bobby Moore – Terry wouldn't be the quickest either – but for Chelsea there has been a real touch of greatness about him. Despite all his personal problems, when you judge what he has done on the pitch, you see a player of outstanding qualities. With Terry there were no excuses, no nonsense about 'Bolton being a tough place to go'. Along with Frank Lampard, even in his younger days, Terry has driven Chelsea in a way that Wayne Rooney, for example, has not driven Manchester United since he became a senior player.

In a much different way, Gianfranco Zola had also been terrific for Chelsea. I wouldn't quite put him up there with Johan Cruyff, but he was a very, very good player. And Didier Drogba in his own peculiar way was a powerful influence. Clearly he has damaged his reputation with his extraordinary carry-on feigning injury and so forth, and on the international front the Ivory Coast have never really done much in the World Cup, and yet for Chelsea he really has been great – strong, quick, good on both sides, aggressive enough. It is just a pity he is also such a big baby. There is no doubt that those histrionics have influenced people's opinion of him as a player. Otherwise he is top notch. When Chelsea needed goals, and needed them badly, he delivered. These were big goals, at home and in Europe. Drogba wouldn't be one of those players who would score the fifth goal in a 5–0 win, he scored at crucial times during Chelsea's run to the final of the Champions League in 2012, and, fittingly enough, under the greatest pressure, he knocked in the winning penalty in the shootout.

Now that Drogba's career in top-class football has ended, we have that perspective. We are only at the start of what may be a new era in the Premier League in which Manchester City are the dominant force, with Sergio Aguero, David Silva, Yaya Touré and Vincent Kompany already doing great things for City, which I hope they can continue to do.

Jack Wilshere at Arsenal has the potential to become a genuine midfield player for his club and for England, maybe the only one of his generation. And Gareth Bale with his outstanding ability and pace has already established himself as a star of the Premier League – the challenge now is to sustain it. Meanwhile at United, a lot depends on the future direction of the career of Wayne Rooney. And while it used to be taken for granted that it would have a happy ending, at this point I have my doubts. We just don't know any more – all we know for certain is that Rooney's performance in Euro 2012 was not that of a great player, nor was his performance at the 2010 World Cup, and since he became the top man at Manchester United, Rooney has gone backwards in his quest for greatness. There is no doubt whatsoever that he has the ability to be one of the immortals, and that in the early parts of his career with his tremendous attitude he showed all the signs of getting there. But there is no doubt either that we have been looking at someone who, at the age of twenty-six or twenty-seven, should be pushing on to that next level, but who hasn't been doing it.

Maybe his rise to a more senior role at Manchester United has been contributing to the problem. It should be a natural thing, as a player develops and matures. But I feel there is a culture at United, which started in the time of Eric Cantona and continued with Cristiano Ronaldo, that if you were considered the top dog, you could indulge yourself, and you would be indulged. But that was all right in the cases of Cantona and Ronaldo, simply because it worked. And part of the reason it worked with Ronaldo was that Rooney was working so hard, playing wide on the left or on the right. His attitude at the time was exemplary, winning the ball back, using it well if he had it, even though he was not playing in his best position. He was giving everything for the team, allowing Ronaldo to do his thing in whatever way he saw fit.

But when Rooney himself assumed the Ronaldo or the Cantona role, becoming the top man, I don't think he was working nearly as hard at his game, particularly when the opposition had the ball. Maybe he became more content in himself, maybe he is influenced by events outside the game, I don't know, and frankly I don't care about that stuff. All I do know is what I have been looking at on the pitch, which is someone who is not becoming the great player he should be. As we have seen, there are all sorts of reasons why this can happen with different people. If a player is going to fulfil his potential, he should be able to maintain his appetite for the game, regardless of the vast amounts of money sloshing around him. But that is easier said than done, which makes the achievement of those who manage it all the more admirable.

The thing about being a pro that Rooney has to realise is that not only do you have to keep working, you have to work harder to become a Charlton or a Pelé. You must be looking to improve from match to match. They say that a player reaches his peak at about twenty-eight, but just because you have reached the age of twenty-eight doesn't mean you have actually reached your peak. If you don't work at it, you've already reached your peak at twenty-four. If you don't go forwards in football, you go backwards.

Fernando Torres has also taken a few wrong turns on the way to the Hall of Fame. But his journey has been different to that of Rooney. His is the classic case of the striker who is desperately searching for confidence, and becoming increasingly anxious as he fails to find it. And all the circumstances have combined to make it more difficult. He had been at home at Liverpool, where he couldn't stop scoring, until the whole club began to unravel for reasons beyond his control. Then he was not just a striker out of form, he was a huge signing who went to Chelsea at a time when that club was in a bit of a mess. The spotlight was on him, making it harder still for him to regain that fragile thing called confidence. I never thought that Torres was a genuine all-round footballer, so if he is not scoring, he can look quite poor. But Torres does seem to be a grafter, and his attitude suggests he will keep going until the magic comes back.

By comparison with these troubled men, when we look back at a player such as Alan Shearer in the early days of the Premier League, it seems that we are returning to a bygone age, a simpler time. And yet in his own way, Shearer was a peculiar sort of lad. It is said that he turned down Manchester United not once but twice, for which I admire him in a way – he had a mind of his own, he didn't go with the flow. But it meant that he didn't enjoy a lot of the success he would undoubtedly have achieved there, and we can only guess at the acclaim he would have received if he had been a part of a side that was challenging for the Premiership and the Champions League every year.

What we know for sure is that Shearer was a genuine

player. I think the same can be said of his BBC colleague Gary
Lineker, who also scored a lot of goals, was very quick and
very brave. But Shearer was better, and his record at Newcastle
was terrific in a team that never won anything. He was better,
too, than his Newcastle team-mate David Ginola, though
Ginola was one of those players with a particular place in the
game — he was in the 'star' bracket. Because he was a good
dribbler, and very attractive on the ball, it was natural that he
would always appeal to certain supporters and to the press.
And I have always maintained that the game needs stars of
this kind. Though with Ginola it began to reach somewhat
comical proportions when he was made Footballer of the
Year in 1999, his nearest rival for that coveted title being Roy
Keane, who had won the Treble that year with United.

Jürgen Klinsmann was the Footballer of the Year in 1995,
something that was not so strange. Klinsmann was top class,
and not just for that outstanding season he had with Spurs —
he had already won the World Cup with Germany in 1990,
when they were managed by Beckenbauer. Klinsmann was a
very intelligent player, he was mobile, a finisher who knew
what he was doing.

Shearer also had a good knowledge of the game, and that
unusual career of his lasted a long time. It is fascinating to
think what he might have done in the same team as Peter
Schmeichel, Paul Scholes and Roy Keane, because they
achieved greatness, and in that company Shearer would have
had a better chance of achieving it himself. But he wanted more
than anything else to be the Newcastle number nine, which is
a magical thing for anyone from that part of the world, the

shirt worn by Hughie Gallacher and Jackie Milburn. We all have our dream, it is the dream that drives you. And though these are cynical times, in his own stubborn way, Shearer held on to his dream and made it come true.

That is no small reward.

13

Barcelona

We have moved from a time in which football men would argue in pubs about the qualities of players they had never seen, to a time in which you can see a game on television most nights of the week, not just in the English leagues but all across Europe and beyond. No longer do we have to wait for months or even years to see the great players in a European Cup final or at the World Cup. Compared to when I was playing, the pitches are in beautiful condition and the facilities at the grounds are so much better. By attracting a more middle-class following, the audience for football has increased greatly. The dangers are also much different. In my playing days, the game was not just more physical, it was over-physical, and

I was one of the culprits. Now the problem is not so much players being injured, as players pretending to be injured, and generally trying to fool the referees by diving and all sorts of 'simulation', as they call it. I think this has become very, very harmful to the game.

And it remains a danger because no one has taken responsibility for it. You would hear Sir Alex Ferguson saying that we need to cut out the diving, and who was his star player? Ronaldo. You would hear José Mourinho saying the same thing and who did he have leading the line? Drogba. They've had a few divers at Arsenal too, but Wenger never saw anything. Recently I heard the Stoke manager Tony Pulis saying that diving was 'creeping into the game'. I'm afraid to say, Tony, that it has been established for the past five years for all to see. It is putting more pressure on referees, who already find themselves in all sorts of ridiculous positions, not all of their own making. According to the FA, a referee may be as infallible as the Pope, because if he sees something that happens on the pitch, and he takes no action at the time, no further action can be taken. In these situations the referee is a protected species, who can't be wrong – even when he *is* wrong.

But the game keeps evolving, as we have seen, and hopefully the diving will eventually go the way of the muddy pitches and the maximum wage. We have looked at many of these changes in the game along the way but, in the end, we are back where we started – with the players. We can see them playing all the time now, not like my father and the football men of his time, with their fiercely argued theories about Matthews and Finney. We saw Zinedine Zidane playing for

Real Madrid most Saturday or Sunday nights, and we could see how exceptional he was. Zidane was the first great player I saw who played in this position that is called 'the hole'. It is a very awkward position, just off the centre-forward. So Zidane would not play like a genuine midfield player. He often had to play with his back to goal. But because of his strength and his excellent technique, he was able to protect the ball. It takes a lot of ability to play in that position, or at least to play as well as Zidane did. He had a good shot, and he scored his fair share of goals, including the decisive goals in a Champions League final and in a World Cup final with a French team that also had outstanding players such as Marcel Desailly, Lilian Thuram and Bixente Lizarazu. We hadn't really seen anyone like Zidane before.

Raúl was also a wonderful player for Real Madrid, a tremendous goal scorer. He was a smooth sort of a player, reminiscent of Jimmy Greaves. He looked so smooth because he was well balanced, with good control, one of those left-footed players who somehow give the appearance of being more stylish on the ball than those who favour the right. All round, Raúl was probably not quite as good as Greaves, but then very few have been.

Luis Figo was another top player who, against the fashion of the times, did most of his stuff on the right wing. He could do this because he was very strong, with good skill and vision, a real footballer. He had to be top class to do such damage in that position, in his time. And there is no doubt that his fellow Portuguese star Cristiano Ronaldo does a huge amount of damage, of the right kind, in his own way. I would always have the highest regard for his ability and his incredible scoring record, yet the viewers of RTÉ will know by now how I feel about Ronaldo – that he does things that the great players do, but he also does things that the great players would never do. His supporters seem to think that those of us who acknowledge his immense talent but who have these reservations about him in some way take pleasure from it – so why do we not take the same pleasure in having reservations about Lionel Messi? The fact that we're talking about these issues at all suggests that, at this stage, you can't really put Ronaldo up there with Messi. Nor are there any reservations of any kind about Iker Casillas, a truly great goalkeeper and in his quiet way an inspirational leader for Real Madrid and for Spain.

For a while Real Madrid also had Ronaldo of Brazil who, to me, never, ever looked fit. But what a goal scorer. He was quick, he could dribble and he was a great finisher. But as for being a great player, you'd have to say he was another could-have-been. You have to imagine what he could have been like if he was dedicated, or even if he was physically fit most of the time. I think he would have achieved true greatness if he had looked after himself. His compatriot Ronaldinho was absolutely brilliant too for a certain period with Barcelona, and yet instead of pushing on, he became another of those players who seemed to say to themselves, 'I've done enough.'

At Barcelona, under Pep Guardiola, there would be no such thing as 'I've done enough.' You could never do enough, you could never bask in self-satisfaction before the job was truly finished. You could always strive to get better. And that is how it should be. The only time you are entitled to bask in that

Charlie Hurley, Sunderland and Ireland legend. A colossus.

Tony Dunne, less celebrated than Best, Law, and Charlton, but vital to United's success.

Frank Stapleton, excellent player who worked his way to the top.

Liam Brady, wonderful style and an absolute pleasure to play alongside.

Kevin Moran, an absolute credit to himself and the game.

Paul McGrath, phenomenon.

Ray Houghton epitomised the success of the new 'granny-rule'.

Packie (Patrick) Bonner, an Irish hero.

Roy Keane, the antithesis of a 'sunshine boy', and the player you would most want on your team if your life depended on it.

Robbie Keane, record goal-scorer and top-class servant to the Republic.

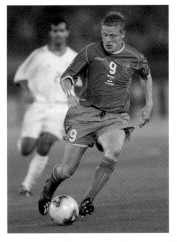

Damien Duff, a great credit to Irish football.

Shay Given, Ireland's best-ever keeper.

Alf Ramsey, man of few words, great manager.
With (l to r) Barry Bridges, Jack Charlton and Nobby Stiles.

Don Revie (left) and Bill Shankly,
great rivals but friends.

Brian Clough, man of many words,
brilliant manager.

Jock Stein, Scottish genius.

Alex Ferguson. Incredible.

way is when you've finished playing and you know that you reached your potential. And even then, you will not find the great players basking in self-satisfaction.

Barcelona have set the standards in recent years. And it has been great for football overall, not just for Barcelona and, by extension, for Spain. Because of that copycat effect in football, they have had an influence on younger coaches, in the right way. And one of the main attractions is that this way of playing the game has been wonderfully successful.

It can look simple, but then all the great performers, the great artists in any field, have that ability to make it look simple. Barcelona can make it look pretty easy and fairly normal to keep the ball for twenty passes, but then you suddenly see England struggling to keep the ball for three passes and you realise how good those guys are. As for the accusations that they are 'boring', you can hardly dignify it with any response, though it is interesting that the great Liverpool teams were often described as 'boring', because they too kept the ball and apparently were 'going nowhere with it' – but somehow they won nearly every match they played.

We are accustomed to the Premier League, where it might be argued that a team such as Barcelona could be bullied out of it – 'They wouldn't fancy it up at Stoke'. But then who would? And it is true that Xavi and Iniesta and Fabregas and Messi are not big, bulky guys. They are not considered box-to-box players, the physical type, and all those other words that are bandied about by those who find Barcelona boring.

But then, when I played the game, I never considered myself small. I was short, which is quite a different thing. So I see these 'small' Barcelona players and I realise that some of them are probably as strong as Jack Charlton in certain ways, around the legs, for example. You never see Xavi or Lionel Messi being shrugged off the ball. They have the advantage of a low centre of gravity that, say, Andy Carroll doesn't have. And they also have the touch, the passing ability, the imagination. A short fellow can just avoid physical contact anyway, because he has these other talents.

It used to be said that 'you have to kick your way out of the Second Division'. But I believe that, inspired by Barcelona, coaches such as Brendan Rodgers and Paul Lambert have been finding more creative ways to survive and to make progress. Even Ian Holloway at Blackpool was converted. Just as some of the coaches of the 1980s followed a pretty horrible model, these days we are seeing the spread of a true football philosophy.

Pep Guardiola, influenced by the original ideas brought to Barcelona by Johan Cruyff, was the guardian of that philosophy, and his players subscribed to it with total dedication. And they are great players – Lionel Messi, Xavi Hernandez, Andrés Iniesta and Cesc Fabregas could have played in any of the great teams, be it Brazil in Mexico, Liverpool of the 1970s, the Dutch teams of the late 1960s and early 1970s. David Villa is a great goal scorer. Carles Puyol and Gerard Piqué are very good, and from what we have seen of his performances for Spain in Euro 2012, Jordi Alba looks a cracker.

When they have the ball, they hold on to it with that understated brilliance that you only appreciate when you see others not being able to do it. And when they don't have the ball, these great players work as hard as any ordinary player would to get it back. The result, for their opponents, is hell. The Barcelona attitude is that if we make it hell for the other team, they won't make it hell for us. And if they do, we can take it.

We are back again to first principles, to time and space. The pitch is of a certain size. You have to use that space. The great players create their own space out there, each time they touch the ball. If you get an ordinary player, and you guarantee him ten square yards of space every time he gets the ball, he will be almost as good as Xavi. But the hard part is creating that space. And in creating their own space, Barcelona also deny space to the opposition. In another strange echo of Jack Charlton, we can say that they 'put 'em under pressure'. We saw in Euro 2012 in the England–Italy game that England couldn't keep the ball because Italy worked so hard to deny them space. And yet when Italy came up against Spain in the final, they were totally outplayed. Spain did to Italy what Italy had done to England. Because now Spain could keep the ball, and work just as hard. That is how the best teams emerge. In the Champions League final of 2011, Manchester United could keep up the pressure against Barcelona for about fifteen minutes at the most. But Barcelona are relentless. And ninety minutes is a long time out there. To keep up the pressure for the first fifteen minues is fine, but for the last fifteen minutes of the game, United were being slaughtered. Those minutes are just as important.

I love Barcelona doing what they do, and the fact that they are so successful doing it. You can set them up as an example all the time. If they weren't winning, people would be suggesting that they need a big fellow to knock it up to, or whatever. But they stick to their philosophy, which takes a great deal of courage. I have seen them 1–0 down, still holding to their beliefs, never punting the ball. We keep hearing that when Plan A doesn't work for Barcelona, they have no Plan B. But the big plan is to hold on to the ball, and to win the ball back quickly when they've lost it. Either you have the ball or you don't have it. When you don't have it, everyone is obliged to make an honest effort to win it back. And when you have the ball, everyone is obliged to use it as conctructively as they possibly can. That sometimes means that the big centre-half has to kick it into Row Z. But if Piqué is on the edge of his own box, and he can give a ten-yard pass to Xavi, he is obliged to do that. By sending Piqué up to centre-forward in the last few minutes and punting it up to him in the desperate search for a late goal, for every one game in which you might get something, there'll be ten in which you won't. And, anyway, if you can set aside your plan like that, you won't be as committed to it. The whole reason that Barcelona have been so successful is that they didn't change from Plan A, despite the fact that very occasionally, they will lose a game. At which point, for the critics, everything is wrong.

In that amazing Champions League semi-final against Chelsea, we saw once again that football is ultimately a game of chance. When you play as many matches as Barcelona do, eventually you'll get a couple of games when it goes against you. Chelsea showed courage in defending well, and the gamble paid off for them with Barcelona missing chances, hitting the post, and even Messi missing a penalty. That is the game. I was lucky enough to play in a Leeds team full of great players, who went through an entire First Division campaign losing only two matches, one of which was a 5–1 defeat by Burnley. An unbelievable result on all known form, but it happened. On any given day, the big centre-half hits one from thirty-five yards into the top corner. You will always get great shocks in sport, that is part of the magic. It shows us again how fragile success can be. But the great managers like Guardiola, Shankly or Busby, because of their knowledge, their organisation and the great players they have acquired, reduce that element of uncertainty as much as they possibly can.

We hear so much about tactics and about formations but, at the 2012 European Championship, the first question that the Spanish manager Vicente del Bosque asked himself was the right question – who are my best players? He put the players at his disposal before any tactical plan. The players, by their ability, made the plan. And just to see them passing the ball to each other – there's nothing tactical about that, it doesn't involve holding forth about 4–3–3 or 4–4–2. But it's a start. At Euro 2012, Spain played a formation never seen before but it didn't matter. They had the players to do it, many of them Barcelona players, all of them playing like Barcelona. And the way Barcelona do it has moved the game on to another level. It is at once immensely sophisticated, and at a more important level it is utterly simple.

This is the game that we learned in the streets. This is the game that we love.

14

Dedicated to the Republic

The Republic of Ireland had had some outstanding players before I arrived, and quite a few after me as well. But again I can't speak with any authority about the former, except to say that a player such as Jackie Carey, who captained Manchester United when they won the FA Cup in 1948 and the league in 1952 and who was Footballer of the Year in 1949, was by all accounts a great player. He was a boyhood hero of mine and, as such, an influence on me. But it is better to start with the players I actually played with, from my debut for Ireland in 1959 onwards.

No better place to start, indeed, than with two men who

impressed me greatly from the first moment I met them, Charlie Hurley and Noel Cantwell. Apart from anything else, they looked like movie stars to me, and, in fact, when you'd see them with Pat Saward, another Irish international at the time, you would think that three Hollywood legends and not three footballers from Cork had somehow showed up in the dressing room at Dalymount Park.

Thankfully they could play. Charlie Hurley was one of the best ever Irish players, often described as a colossus, and rightly so. Unusually for a colossus, he also had really good feet. The centre-halves of the time were generally just big guys whose job it was to kick the centre-forward up in the air. They were a rough and ready crowd, and Charlie was aggressive too, without being a dirty player. He was brilliant in the air, but he'd also want to play it out from the back, and with his ability, he could do that. With his power in the air, he could score goals when he came up for corners, a bit like John Terry. In fact, Charlie was one of the best headers of a ball I have ever seen.

He moved from Millwall to Sunderland, where he was eventually voted Sunderland's Player of the Century by the fans. I know that some of these polls can be silly, but it does give some indication of how highly he is regarded – especially given that Sunderland is an area with such a rich tradition, full of football people who are really passionate about the game. Though he played for them in the late 1950s and 1960s, when Charlie goes back to Sunderland all these years later, he still gets a great reception. And this despite the fact that during his time at the club, they didn't win anything.

When I went to Leeds, we had a big rivalry with Sunderland, and both of us were promoted together after the 1963–1964 season. Charlie went on to spend much of the 1960s at Roker Park before moving on to Bolton Wanderers. But it wasn't his long career in England that removed any trace of an Irish accent from Charlie – he never had an Irish accent in the first place. He was born in Cork, but his family had moved to Rainham in Essex when he was just a few months old. If you met him, you would assume he was a real Cockney.

The aforementioned Pat Saward was another of the 'Cork' players with an English accent, for the obvious reason that he was brought up in Newmarket. Which goes to show that Andy Townsend and Tony Cascarino were by no means the first players for the Republic who didn't sound very 'Irish'.

Noel Cantwell, though, was not just born in Cork, he sounded every bit of it. He and Charlie were already idols of mine when I played with them in my first international in 1959 against Sweden at Dalymount Park. And while they say you should never meet your heroes, on this occasion it went very well, with Noel as captain a particular help to me on the day. His personality was such that he would take control of things in a natural way. He would come over and talk to you, tell you not to be nervous. It is a quality called leadership, and Noel had it.

He was a very, very good player, a big fellow at left-back who was always constructive. He was a good distributor of the ball, who could 'dink it into the centre-forward', as we say. Noel had a good mind about the game, he wanted to contribute in that way. Which is not something that every player does. Tony Dunne, for example, was a terrific player for Manchester United and Ireland, but Tony's personality was basically different to Noel's. He would tend to look after his own game. Noel was more the type who wanted to give advice, to get involved in everything.

I eventually played in the same club team as Noel when he joined Manchester United in 1960 from West Ham United, where he had been captain. For various reasons, I don't think that Noel did himself justice at Manchester United. He had got a very bad throat infection during his early days there, which seemed to linger for a long time, and he had other injuries too. He had come in from the outside in more ways than one, arriving quite late in his career from West Ham, where a lot of the modern ideas about coaching were coming in. The likes of Malcolm Allison, John Bond and Malcolm Musgrove all went into management, fired up with this new thinking, but Matt Busby was one of the old-style managers. He brought the right players to the club – Noel was signed for almost £30,000, a record for a full-back – but then he tended to let the players get on with it. And this was probably strange to Noel. A lot of the Busby Babes were still there too, reinforcing this feeling of being an outsider.

And though he captained the FA Cup-winning team of 1963, I don't think Noel really embraced the Busby way. His time at United was not as productive as it might have been, not as good as his time at West Ham had been anyway. That said, he was a big servant for the Republic, captaining the team and becoming joint-manager for a while with Charlie Hurley, who would take over from him as captain. Noel actually served his country in two sports, as he had played a few games of international cricket for Ireland along the way.

Tony Dunne, as I said, was more of a quiet type of lad. And as a schoolboy player, he had been a relatively late developer. In fact, he was in the same schoolboy year as myself, but he did not get onto the schoolboy international team. Most lads who eventually achieved what Tony did in the game would have been outstanding at schoolboy level, but Tony came on late. He played, along with Eric Barber, with a good youth team, St Finbarr's, who were rivals of my team, Stella Maris. And he went on from Finbarr's to play with Shelbourne in the League of Ireland. Now at eighteen, Tony was much better than a lot of the players who had been ahead of him when they were fifteen. It just happens that certain players develop in this way, while others fall back.

He was playing regularly for Shels when Manchester United signed him. It was just after the Munich disaster, and Tony came on very quickly, getting into the first team. He became one of the outstanding full-backs in the First Division for the next ten years. The 1960s in general was not the best of times for the Republic in terms of producing players, with the old Selection Committee still in place and a run-down system meaning that almost anyone could have got a cap for Ireland. But Tony Dunne was a really top-class player.

He was perhaps not as good a distributor of the ball as Noel Cantwell, but he was quicker, well balanced, and very good in the air for his size. He was one of those defenders who win it and serve it, who get on with the job quietly. The sort who went almost unnoticed in a team with an international superstar like George Best in it, but who still played a vital part in United's success.

Part of the reason why Tony Dunne did not get the recognition he deserved was the very fact that he played for the Republic, and thus had a much lower profile than a player who might be nowhere near as good but who got a few caps for England. Which made a big difference. Indeed in those days when players were not automatically released for international matches, it was easy for the top English clubs to prevent their players travelling for internationals, which meant that Tony would have missed out on several caps.

He might not have been a great mixer, but when a few of us had our meeting to demand that the FAI change more or less everything it was doing, Tony was there. In fact, he was the one who raised the idea of a doctor travelling with us for away matches. Amazing though it now seems, we did not have the brilliant medical team that the Republic has at present – in fact, we did not have any kind of a doctor on trips abroad. As a senior player, Tony was aware of these deficiencies.

From the mid-1960s, the Republic could also call on the services of the other full-back at Manchester United, Shay Brennan. He was the first English-born player to take advantage of the parentage rule, and though Shay was born and raised in Manchester, he said that he always felt Irish. He spent a lot of summer holidays back in Ireland as a kid, and had a genuine affection for the place. We were also delighted to have him, because Shay was a good lad and a good player, a top-class player in fact, one of the few we have had who won a European Cup medal. He also won two league titles with United in 1965 and 1967.

Shay was about three years older than me when I was at United. He was one of the Busby Babes, who had started out as an inside-forward but who wasn't quite doing it there. He did better when he moved to half-back, and then he found his best position when he moved to full-back. A similar thing had happened with Jackie Carey, himself a really good footballer who made the move backwards into defence, but who still had the creative instincts of a midfield player. In general, the farther forward you are, the harder it is to play. For example, as a forward, with your back to goal, the difficult thing is getting turned around to get at the opposition. But the farther back you go, the more you are facing the play, and so you can use all your abilities as an inside-forward without that problem of getting turned round on the ball.

This is how Shay Brennan made his way into that great United team, and Shay, being a very modest individual, talked about how privileged he felt to be playing alongside players of the stature of Bobby Charlton, Denis Law and George Best. Shay played for Ireland nineteen times in the worst of the bad old days, when the lads were still coming over on the boat to play on Sunday after playing for thir clubs on the Saturday, and when the Big Five of the FAI were still picking the team. But he still felt honoured to play for Ireland. In fairness, most international football in the 1940s and 1950s had been run in this ramshackle way, but in other countries they had started to change in the 1960s. England had finally done the right thing in 1963 and appointed Alf Ramsey to manage the team properly. But it would take a few years for that change to come for the Republic.

Another player who soldiered on during those years when it wasn't fashionable or even pleasant was Eamon Dunphy. As most readers are probably aware, Eamon is very self-deprecating about his playing career in general and about the twenty-three international caps he got. So it needs to be said that Eamon was what we call 'a footballer'. Which is a high compliment. He was coming from the same place that Liam Brady and I were coming from, playing in the streets, the best place to develop your instincts for the game. Eamon knew when to deliver a pass, when to hold on to it, when to put pace on the ball.

He jokes a lot about playing for Millwall, which was obviously on a lower level than Manchester United where he started. And yet Millwall at the time, though they were in the Second Division, were a very good Second Division team, featuring the likes of Keith Weller, Harry Cripps, Barry Kitchener and Derek Possee. Notoriously, they thought they had won promotion to the First Division in 1971–1972, and were celebrating on the pitch at The Den when the word came through that a late header by Bob Latchford at Leyton Orient had put Birmingham City up instead, denying Millwall promotion by one point. Latchford's goal came from a corner taken by Gordon Taylor, now the Chief Executive of the Professional Footballers' Association, and Latchford went on to become one of the top goal scorers in the First Division in the 1970s.

At Millwall, Eamon was a 'schemer', as they were called at the time. The equivalent today would be the more talented type of midfield player, the one who isn't 'sitting' or 'holding' but who has a more creative role.

He actually made his international debut in one of our most important games of that era, the play-off against Spain at a 'neutral' venue in Paris, which Spain won 1–0 to qualify for the 1966 World Cup. He had the skill and the temperament to handle that occasion.

Don Givens, who came along towards the end of the 1960s, was a more quietly spoken individual who still said his piece when the time was right. And he could also take the mickey, in a quiet way. He too had gone to Manchester United, but it didn't work out for him there, and so he went to Luton Town – Don was another late-comer who was maturing as he left Luton for Queens Park Rangers, where he was rightly recognised as a top-class striker for several seasons in the First Division. On the international front, he became Ireland's record goal scorer until Niall Quinn. Don was quick, a good header of the ball, an intelligent player with an eye for goal. He was clever in the timing of his runs. He would not be like, say, Andy Carroll, coming in at the back post. His style was more to sneak in front of defenders, getting into the right position at the right time, making it look easy. He read the game well.

Don scored nineteen goals for the Republic, but his best-known performance was his famous hat-trick against the USSR at Dalymount Park in October 1974. It was during my time as player-manager, and a certain level of expectation had built up, which was very strange for any Irish team. It had started from my first match in charge when we beat Poland 1–0 at home. Then there was a tour of South America in which we had surprised everyone by playing well against Brazil, losing 2–1 in the Maracana. We had played disappointingly against Uruguay, losing 2–0, but we had finished on a high by beating a very useful Chile side 2–1. So we took it as a compliment that people now thought we could put up a decent display against the Soviet Union in a European Championship qualifier. There was the added excitement that it was eighteen-year-old Liam Brady's first match for the Republic. And it turned out to be a glorious day, the three goals scored by Don illustrating all his attributes – his power in the air, the excellent runs that he made and his intelligence. He went on to score another four goals in the home game against Turkey, our last competitive game in Dalymount before the move to Lansdowne Road. That defeat of the USSR remains one of the great occasions in the Republic's football history, certainly one of the most fondly remembered. Something about the atmosphere in Dalymount, the brilliance of Liam in his debut, and of course the win against one of the game's superpowers made it really special. And Don Givens was at the centre of it.

Steve Heighway was another late developer, so late that he had even managed to get a university degree in politics and economics before he was discovered playing for Skelmersdale United by a Liverpool scout. With Shankly rebuilding at the time, Heighway was given his chance and was hailed as a hero more or else straight away by the Anfield crowd. Naturally he had no problem bursting onto the scene for the Republic, where we were always rebuilding. And especially when you consider that at the time, anyone who could play at all would be capped immediately – in those days, you would not be kept waiting for your international debut the way James McClean or James McCarthy are today. So if you were as good as Steve Heighway, who was born in Dublin, you were drafted in straight away.

He was a very good player, really top class, though perhaps he did not embrace the Republic as much as Shay Brennan did, or like the lads who came later such as Chris Hughton, Ray Houghton or Andy Townsend. He was something of a loner, who did not really mix much with the other Irish lads. But Steve could play. He was an out-and-out left-winger, who could dribble it off his right foot, who could come inside or drag it down the line, and he was very quick. He had become a star at Liverpool before Kevin Keegan arrived, and he would be part of the team that went on to become so successful in that period, driven by Keegan. Steve eventually picked up thirty-four caps for the Republic at various times throughout the 1970s. He was probably one of the best players who played for us.

The same could be said of goalkeeper Alan Kelly – in fact, I would say that Alan was our best keeper by far, until Packie Bonner came along, and then Shay Given. At Deepdale, the home of Preston North End where Alan spent his entire English career, there is a stand named after him. The Alan Kelly Stand even has a design of his face, made up by the different coloured seats. And if that is not enough of an indication of the esteem in which he is held, it should be noted that the other stand is named after Sir Tom Finney. Originally from Bray – he started out with Bray Wanderers – Alan was still playing for Drumcondra when he was capped against

England in a World Cup qualifier at Wembley in 1957. It was an unusual move for a young League of Ireland player to be thrown in to such a big match, and probably his selection was a bit premature. Alan had a bad day at Wembley and was out of the international team for a few years – he wasn't in goal in 1959 when I made my debut. But pretty soon he had established himself at Preston as a really top-class keeper. And, to say the least, the Republic needed one of them.

A good goalkeeper is always a tremendous asset on a number of levels, and a vital neccessity even in a very good team. At a time when the Republic needed a good goalkeeper more than most, Alan was terrific. I know that most keepers are supposed to be a bit bonkers, but Alan wasn't that type. He had a good knowledge of the game, which meant that his judgement of when to come out, and when not to, was first class. As a result, you didn't see him making many bad mistakes. A keeper who lacks that judgement will always just be guessing about when to come, and when not to come. So on average he'll be right 50 per cent of the time and wrong the other 50 per cent. That was not Alan's way at all, and he wasn't just astute in his reading of a situation, he was also a great shot-stopper.

Often these days, you will hear a keeper being described as a great shot-stopper, but a bit lacking in judgement. In the case of Alan Kelly, and the many other good keepers in England at that time, both of these attributes were basic requirements. Alan had plenty of shots to stop for the Republic over the years, plenty of fine judgements to make. And we were very lucky to have him there. Indeed I regard it as unfortunate for me that when I took over as manager, I couldn't call on Alan, because he had picked up a shoulder injury which eventually ended his career.

Which is not to take away at all from the contribution of Mick Kearns, who did his stuff for us in goal when we needed him. Mick would be the first to say that he was no Alan Kelly, but Mick was a terrific lad who served the Republic well both as a player and as a very popular member of the squad. For soldiering on during the bad days, honourable mentions should also go to Noel Campbell, Noel Peyton, Ronnie Nolan, Gerry Daly, Mick McGrath, Andy McEvoy, Tony Grealish and Dave Langan. And there was Joe Haverty, who, like Mick McGrath, was playing for Ireland when I made my debut.

Joe went from St Patrick's Athletic to Arsenal and was an immediate star at Highbury. He was one of those small, tricky wingers who was able to zip past the big, old-fashioned full-backs. Nor are we forgetting the contributions of those who were best known as League of Ireland players, men such as Eamonn Gregg, Frank O'Neill, Noel Synnott, Alan O'Neill, Ray and Fran O'Brien, Paul Magee from Sligo, Turlough O'Connor from Athlone, Alfie Hale and Peter Fitzgerald from Waterford, Al Finucane from Limerick and Miah Dennehy from Cork.

Alfie Hale was signed by Aston Villa in 1960, when Villa were having a bad time. As a result, I don't think it was a happy time for Alfie either, and he moved to Doncaster Rovers for whom he scored forty-two goals in three seasons. But he came back to Waterford and he never had any regrets about it. I don't think Alfie had any great ambition to go to England anyway.

But he was a very good player – quick, with good control, and he scored a lot of goals for Waterford during their highly successful period in the 1960s. In different circumstances, I think he could have made it in England.

Peter Fitzgerald was also from a well-known family of footballers in Waterford. He had spells at Leeds United and Chester City in the early 1960s, and he played five times for Ireland. Al Finucane also gave good service to the Republic. Al was a centre-back, a good-hearted lad who gave everything he had. For a long time he was one of the leading players in the League of Ireland with Limerick and Waterford, but he never went to England, though several clubs including Everton were said to be interested in signing him. Miah Dennehy was signed by Nottingham Forest for £20,000 in 1973, but he will always be best remembered for his hat-trick for Cork Hibernians in the FAI Cup final of 1972, and for his eleven appearances for Ireland.

Jim Beglin, whose career was sadly cut short by a broken leg, was another Waterford man. It was actually Eamon Dunphy who saw Jim playing in Waterford, which resulted in Jim joining Shamrock Rovers when he was seventeen. Jim was a smashing lad. Even as a kid you could see that he had a really professional attitude. When he signed for Liverpool, it was no surprise that he fitted in so well there, and that he was good enough to play for the Liverpool team that won the Double in 1985–1986.

Mick Meagan played at full-back for the Everton team that won the league in 1963. Mick was a good footballer who played wing-half for Ireland and who became the first manager of the Republic after the demise of the Selection Committee. When I became manager, I took over from Liam Tuohy, who had left the job for personal reasons. Liam had been a top-class player with Shamrock Rovers in the Paddy Coad era, and he then had a short spell with Newcastle United – a football man through and through.

We were lucky too to have men of the calibre of Paddy Mulligan, Mick Martin, Ray Treacy, Eoin Hand, Terry Conroy and Jimmy Holmes, who were all really good servants in that time before the 'granny rule' was extended. In fact at one point when I was manager, Mick Kearns and Terry Mancini were the only ones in the squad who hadn't been born and reared in Ireland.

Paddy Mulligan was a very intelligent player, who played at right-back and centre-back for me. He had gone from Shamrock Rovers to Chelsea, then Crystal Palace, and from there he came to West Bromwich Albion when I was player-manager. Paddy became a folk hero at West Brom, and is still a popular figure to this day. Mick Martin also moved from the League of Ireland to the English First Division, from Bohemians to Manchester United. Son of the famous Con, who had also played for Ireland, Mick was similar to Paddy Mulligan in being very intelligent – you would only need to say something once to these guys, and it was understood. Tommy Docherty didn't want to keep Mick at United, but I knew he was a good player so I took him on loan to West Brom, eventually paying £20,000 for him when we decided to keep him, as I knew we would. He played on the right-hand side, could cover the ground well, defend well, get you the odd goal.

Eoin Hand was another good servant to the cause over the years. Centre-half was his natural position, but he played in midfield at the start for me. He could win tackles, making him in today's term a 'holding' player. And there was Ray Treacy, always there for us in the bad days and the good days, always a trier and a very good header of the ball. Terry Conroy was a raider, a winger, a good dribbler who played on the right or the left side when I was manager. Terry was deceptively quick, which could cause problems for any opposition. Jimmy Holmes, too, at left-back was one of the lads who kept it going in those years when we had a bit of a revival. I would still see a few of those lads now and again, and of course I see a lot of of Liam Brady who is a fellow pundit on the RTÉ panel.

I picked Liam for his international debut, but then you didn't need to be a genius to see that he could play. Frank Stapleton and David O'Leary also made their debuts for me, signalling the start of a new phase and a major change for the international team – to put it simply, we now had better players, either home grown like Brady, Stapleton and O'Leary, or drafted in under the 'granny' rule like Mark Lawrenson. They would all become stalwarts of the Republic over the years, and Liam in particular would become one of the great players for any country – he always took pride in playing for Ireland but Liam could have played with Brazil. He would not have looked out of place in any way in their most illustrious teams.

He had a natural balance, and a turn of pace that was very deceptive. Sometimes he seemed to be loping along, taking it easy, but then suddenly there would be that burst of speed.

This allowed him to go past people in tight areas, which in any position on the pitch is an invaluable asset. But if you can do it in midfield, as Liam could, then it is even better, because you are really opening up the play. In these tight areas, you would see other players receiving the ball and being boxed in, whereas with a player of Liam's quality, the more trouble they seem to be in, the more they can produce.

Apart from his great talent on the ball, he had a football brain, which meant that he could deliver a ball at the right time, that he had the vision to see a long pass. He had a good shot in his left foot, he could threaten the goals. In fact, Liam was one of those players of whom it is said, 'You would pay in to watch him' – a bit like the stars of that earlier era in English football, the Wilf Mannions and the Tom Finneys whose performances were appreciated even by the fans of the opposing team. Unfortunately, Liam was playing at a time when there wasn't quite the same generosity of spirit out there, and yet anyone with any real affection for the game loved the way that he played, his beautiful control, that style of his that was so easy on the eye.

Certainly there was no question in my mind about putting him in the team at the earliest opportunity, and as we saw in that game against the USSR, even at eighteen he did not find the occasion too big for him in any shape or form. Liam would have been like me when he went to Dalymount, a Dublin lad who had always dreamed of playing there in big games. The Bradys were a football family, with Liam's brother Frank playing for Shamrock Rovers, another brother Paddy playing for Millwall and QPR, and Ray who also played for Millwall and QPR and who got six caps for Ireland. Indeed we should mention that Ray has a footnote in the history of the Republic as the centre-half on the day in 1963 when Ireland achieved one of its legendary miracle draws – this time a scoreless draw in Vienna against Austria in a qualifier for the European Nations Cup. It was remarkable mainly for the fact that we could hardly get any of the usual players released for the game, so the team featured men such as Willie Browne, an amateur who played for Bohemians, and others who hadn't played for Ireland for years, including Tommy Traynor, Liam Tuohy, Dermot Curtis and Ronnie Whelan Senior. And yet, somehow, we got a draw which helped to knock the Austrians out of the competition, with Ray Brady making a notable contribution, concentrating mainly, shall we say, on the physical side of the game. Ray was clearly dissimilar in style to his young brother Liam, who from the start was a classical player, inventive and creative. But coming from the strong football background that he did, learning the game in the streets in the traditional way, Liam never let it go to his head. Just because he was the star man at Arsenal at a young age, and one of the stars of the English game in general, it did not stop him joining in the sing-song in the hotel after a game at Dalymount with the rest of us – his big number was 'Ruby (Don't Take Your Love To Town)'. It all seems like a very long time ago. These days, I see a lot of professional footballers arriving at a game listening to their own choice of music on headphones, blocking out the world, and I don't suppose they have a party piece that they perform with the lads in the hotel later on.

Sophisticated in all the right ways, in 1980 Liam was signed by Giovanni Trappatoni, then manager of Juventus, for a fee of £500,000, no doubt partly influenced by his performance for Arsenal against Juventus in the semi-final of the Cup Winners' Cup, which Arsenal won 2–1 on aggregate. There are Arsenal fans who are still broken-hearted that Liam moved on, after his Arsenal team had reached three FA Cup finals in a row, winning the one in 1979 against Manchester United with a famous late goal by Alan Sunderland, set up by Liam. But while the sadness of those Arsenal fans at his departure was understandable, there was a sense of pride that they had developed a player of Liam's stature. And as an authentic Arsenal legend, they were happy to see him back at the club when he retired from playing, to work on the youth system. They also knew better than anyone that he was entitled to take his chance at the very highest level – which at that time was the Italian league, which was attracting the top players from all over Europe. For example, when Liam left Juventus after two seasons and two Serie A titles, he was replaced as the main man in midfield by Michel Platini, who had become available from Saint Etienne, and who was, as we know only too well, a good player – a very, very good player – but arguably not a great player in the sense that Liam Brady was.

At Juventus, too, Liam left with the respect and the affection of the fans. Apart from his creative contribution, the record shows that Liam scored a penalty in a 1–0 win against Catanzaro that clinched the league title for Juventus in 1982. It was in so many ways a glorious career, and it was just a shame that the international side of it did not end where it should have done, at Euro '88 and Italia '90. We know that

Liam picked up a suspension before Euro '88, but, in general, Big Jack did not have much use for him. He did not want him to play in the imaginative way that he had always done, and so one of our greatest players – one of the game's greatest players – was effectively made redundant by a so-called 'system'.

If a system can't accommodate an outstanding player, then the sytem is wrong. But Jack's results were still good enough to make his treatment of Liam acceptable to the public, who might not have followed the game too closely until then and who just wanted to enjoy a certain level of success. Liam's old Arsenal colleague David O'Leary was also unlucky in that he did not conform to Jack's vision of how his centre-backs should play. I certainly didn't have any problems with David, going back to his debut against England at Wembley in a friendly in 1976. Still a teenager, he played exceptionally well in a 1–1 draw – he had to be good because he was marking Kevin Keegan on the night. David was quite tall but very well balanced. He was exceptionally quick, read the game well and didn't try to be too clever. And he was intelligent enough to use it simply. Even as a young lad, he was one of the players who raised the standard of the Republic at that time. I always found him a good pro, who looked after himself well and, sure enough, David had a very long and successful career, making a record number of appearances for Arsenal.

The success of Frank Stapleton with Arsenal and Manchester United was perhaps even more notable because Frank was not as naturally gifted as Brady or O'Leary, and yet he eventually became one of the best players in England. He worked really hard, was totally determined to develop himself, and ended up a better centre-forward than most who were around at that time, at any level. Though he does not hold the goal-scoring record, I would say that Frank was probably the best centre-forward the Republic has ever had. He was a natural in that role, very strong in the air, intelligent enough to take up good positions in order to receive the ball. He could hold it up, he could link it up well to bring players into the game, and to get himself into dangerous areas in and around the box.

A centre-forward such as Peter Osgood could perhaps control the ball better than Frank, and look a bit more stylish, but as a general rule, there are a lot of lads who are naturally gifted who don't work as hard as Frank Stapleton did. For him, nothing was too much trouble if it meant he might improve himself. For this reason, I always had a lot of time for Frank. That fierce dedication is something that the great players have. Lionel Messi possesses gifts that are not far away from being supernatural, and yet Messi would work just as hard as Frank Stapleton. That is what makes the difference.

The emergence of Stapleton, O'Leary and Brady might be seen as a long-overdue lucky break for the Republic, but the finding of another young player in 1977 was a stroke of luck which bordered on the freakish. Preparing for a home game against Poland, I was facing the traditional problem of trying to find enough players from wherever I could. I was told by Alan Kelly, who was then my assistant, that they had this young lad at Preston North End who was now eligible to play for Ireland because his grandfather had been born in Waterford. 'If he's any good at all,' I said, 'we'll take him.' I hadn't seen him play, and indeed I had never heard of him, but Alan said, 'I think he's going to be a good player.' Which was more than enough for me to call up this nineteen-year-old defender, Mark Lawrenson.

Mark, who was just a kid, thought it was all perfectly fine, and none of us imagined that, after a few years, Mark would be regarded as one of the Republic's most brilliant acquisitions. By then he had formed a powerful defensive partnership at Liverpool with Alan Hansen, and England officials were going crackers because they had lost one of the best players in the country because of this unfortunate accident. As for Mark himself, he was always happy to play for the Republic, a good lad and a really outstanding player. He was very quick, read the game well, and had a lot of skill for a central defender. He could come out from the back with the ball, join in the play, give it at the right time. Put it like this, Liverpool signed Mark when they were at their peak, and he fitted in straight away.

The best was still to come for Mark when, in 1987, he got the injury that would end his career. I happened to be at the match at Anfield against Wimbledon when Mark went down with nobody near him. He was running with the ball, the next thing he was on the ground. Which is usually a bad sign, suggesting either a bad knee injury or the one that Mark had suffered, an achilles tendon injury. So he, too, missed out on Euro '88 and Italia '90, though he had made one last contribution to the improvement of the Republic – Mark was not the most prolific goal scorer, but against Scotland at Hampden in the qualifying group for Euro '88 he scored from a quickly taken free kick. The match finished 1–0, giving Jack's team a vital boost at the time.

Chris Hughton, who made his own contribution in his quiet way over the years, did make it to that tournament, playing in all three matches in Germany. Chris was a top-class player for Spurs, and I remember him from my time as manager as a good pro who got on with the job, trained well, another fine servant for the Irish team.

We had goalkeepers such as Paddy Roche, Gerry Peyton and Seamus McDonagh who did not let us down, but Packie Bonner, once he had established himself as Ireland's keeper in the mid-1980s, became a very important player for us. He was playing regularly for Celtic at a time when the standard in Scotland was considerably higher than it is today. Packie was big, he had a presence, he was quite a dominating character in goals. I would say that Packie had more presence than the best Irish keeper before him, Alan Kelly. Alan wouldn't have been as big, physically. Packie was also a good kicker of the ball out of his hands, which came in handy in the time of Big Jack. In fact, if we look back at the two goals that Ireland scored in Italia '90, both of them came almost directly from kick-outs by Packie that eventually arrived at the other end of the pitch at the feet of Kevin Sheedy against England and Niall Quinn against the Netherlands. And of course, Packie could be a match-winner at his own end, too, saving the odd penalty. He also had a quality of leadership that you see sometimes in a very good keeper, a sense that he is not just dominating his own area, but driving the team from the back.

Packie suffered a bit when the back-pass rule came in, as

did many keepers who had spent the majority of their careers never needing to kick the ball off the ground. But by then he had already made his contribution to the Republic, and it was a big contribution.

In front of Packie, there was now a choice of several top-class centre-halves, including Paul McGrath, Kevin Moran, Mick McCarthy and David O'Leary – if David was required by Big Jack, which usually he was not. For a while, Mark Lawrenson was still there too. You had players such as Denis Irwin and Steve Staunton coming along at full-back. It has to be said that we had never seen the likes of it before, or since, and that was just the defence. There is absolutely no doubt that Jack had the best selection of players that Ireland has ever had – at various times, he could have had Liam Brady, Ronnie Whelan, Ray Houghton, John Aldridge and Andy Townsend, not forgetting Frank Stapleton who hadn't retired yet. In fact, when I think of the twenty best players that the Republic has ever had, a very high percentage of them would have been playing at some point during the Charlton years.

Kevin Moran was a phenomenon. I try not to overuse that word, but there is really no other word that can adequately describe him. To do what he did – to become a top-class Gaelic footballer and then to adapt to the English game and to become the player he did – was remarkable. He had not gone away to England as a kid at fifteen, which is usually a major disadvantage but in Kevin's case worked quite well. You find that a lot of lads who go over at fifteen can quickly start to take it for granted. Footballers are well known anyway for having a good moan, even the ones who arrive at Manchester

United. I remember playing golf with Kevin when I was living in Vancouver, and him telling me how surprised he had been when he arrived at United to find that some of the lads were not happy with their lot. Coming from an amateur game, Kevin was delighted with what he found at United, the way that everything was laid on. Back in Dublin, as a Gaelic footballer Kevin would have trained at night, which is hard work after you've done your job during the day. So in Manchester, Kevin thought he had gone to heaven. In fact all of us professional footballers, despite our moaning and our insecurities, are living in a sort of heaven, we just don't realise it when we're playing. I probably didn't appreciate it enough, but Kevin loved every part of it.

I saw some of his early games for United, and I didn't think he was going to do it there. He was raw, inexperienced, inclined to 'dive in' at the wrong time. But he was soon looking a lot better. With his attitude and his ability to learn, he became a real pro, certainly by comparison with some of the pros I have known. With that enthusiasm of his, the progress he made was terrific and, having appeared too crude for the First Division at first, he became one of the top central defenders in England. He had guts, as we know, famously taking whatever blows he needed to take for the team. And when you combine that sort of bravery and athleticism with a high level of intelligence and a determination to succeed, you don't need much more. I would have more admiration for what Kevin did than I would have for most of the people I've known in the game.

With Paul McGrath sometimes playing in midfield or even

at full-back, Mick McCarthy became Kevin's most frequent partner at the centre of the defence for the Republic.

Mick was a good, solid, old-fashioned centre-half, who was excellent in the air. He was probably one of the best headers of the ball I've seen, which enabled him to dominate. Like Kevin, he had the right attitude. Mick was a straightforward defender, which was exactly what Jack wanted. Jack wouldn't really want the centre-half to be constructive on the ball, not an all-round footballer like Lawrenson or McGrath or O'Leary. So Mick was his ideal vision in that position. We know that Jack did not embrace David O'Leary, and I am not sure that he would have embraced Mark Lawrenson either if Mark had still been available. He would usually play Paul McGrath, somewhere, but at centre-back it would always ideally be McCarthy and Moran.

Then Steve Staunton came along at left-back, where he had already established himself in a Liverpool side that was still winning things. Which was just about the best recommendation you could have for any player at that time. Steve had a good, natural left foot, and he could distribute the ball well. By the time of the 2002 World Cup, he had moved to centre-half where he would also play very well – the usual centre-half was Kenny Cunningham, and Kenny was a good all-round player who read the game well and used the ball well. But when Staunton was picked, he didn't just fill the gap, he was outstanding in that role. His attitude was beyond question, and his service to the Republic was extraordinary over the years.

As for Paul McGrath, nearly everything about him was

extraordinary. The most basic football widsom, down through
the years, says that unless you really look after yourself, you
are not going to last. The career of Paul McGrath defied
that wisdom and tore up that rulebook in ways that still
seem incredible to me. First of all, he had trouble with his
knees, the sort of permanent trouble that meant he had to
rest them, and nurse them. So he could not train properly
between matches – effectively he didn't train at all. Certainly
Paul seemed like a naturally fit lad, but usually that is not
enough. The problem is that eventually you lose your fitness –
again this is the conventional wisdom which for some strange
reason didn't seem to apply to Paul McGrath.

In fact, I never knew or heard of anyone in the game that
it didn't apply to, except Paul. I know it applied to me. If I
didn't train because I was nursing an injury, the loss of fitness
would always catch up with me. And if Don Revie asked me
to play in those situations, I was always reluctant. I would tell
him that it wasn't a lack of willingness on my part, it was my
belief that I wouldn't be any use to him anyway. I just wasn't
ready to play to the required standard.

Maybe I was also hearing the voice of Matt Busby, who had
kept telling us that 'you only get out of the game what you put
into it'. Of course that was a myth in one way in particular –
if you were playing for Matt, or most of the other managers
of that time, in fairness, no matter what you were putting into
it, you wouldn't be getting a lot out of it financially. Still, the
message stuck with me and I saw very little to contradict it
until Paul came along, not training and still playing most of
the time, playing very well. He continued to do this, not just

until the age of thirty, at which anyone else in that situation would definitely have been found out, but for several years after that – Paul was still playing for Derby County in the Premier League at the age of thirty-seven.

Like Kevin Moran, he had come to the game in England relatively late, but he also left it later than most, despite his non-training regime. And Paul was drinking as well. We have already mentioned players like Jim Baxter and Paul Gascoigne, exceptionally gifted lads who 'didn't look after themselves', as the saying goes. But none of them were still playing very well at the age of thirty-seven. None of them had played consistently well throughout their careers as Paul had done. I live in the Birmingham area, so I know that Paul is still revered by fans of Aston Villa as a legend. They still sing about him at matches. Alex Ferguson may have dispensed with his services to break up the 'drinking club' at United, but it seemed to make no difference at all to Paul's ability to play top-class football for Villa for several years after, making a far greater contribution than many of the lads who did look after themselves.

I knew a lot of fellows who looked after themselves from week to week, but they looked after themselves most of all on the Saturday. In fact, they were always looking after themselves in every situation and, in the end, they lost the plot in terms of what they were looking after themselves for – supposedly it's to make sure you are giving your absolute best to the team, but those lads had gradually lost interest in that side of it. The thing about Paul is that when he played, he really played. Even in the later stages of his career, you'd never say that he looked like he was struggling. On the contrary, he was brilliant, looking fit, alert, all the things you need. You often hear it said that he read the game so well he didn't really have to do much running, but it doesn't matter how well you read the game, you still have to cover the ground. You still have to match Alan Shearer or Gary Lineker. Reading is not everything. Paul seemed to have a low centre of gravity for a big man. You would see him crouched as he tracked an opponent, which meant that he was well balanced, more so than most centre-halves. He was exceptionally quick, good in the air and his close control was very good. He was hugely talented.

Paul defied all the conventions partly because he was a natural player, by which I mean that he felt most at home when he was out on the pitch. I always got the impression that it was a relief for Paul to get out there, to escape from all his problems, the demons he had. He didn't give the ball away much, he could go past players if they got too close to him, he could win a few tackles, retrieve the ball, which meant that at his prime he could have played the 'holding' role of today's game in his sleep. And sometimes I think he could still be playing that role today.

On a personal level, I like Paul, and I don't know anyone who doesn't. He is one of the most modest lads I have met and also one of the most intelligent. I remember him coming out to RTÉ one day, when we were doing the Premiership highlights programme, and I said to him, 'Why don't you come on tonight?' Paul was reluctant. He had been on the radio a while before that, and apparently had dried up. 'Ah, no, I wouldn't fancy that,' he said. But I managed to persuade him to do it anyway, and he turned out to be very good. Sweating a bit at the start, but fine. Talking about the game in general, I think he is very good, very articulate. Certainly there are many others who are far more confident than Paul, who have none of his knowledge.

If he had played for another country like, say, Brazil, I think he would have been a worldwide name. And, like Liam Brady, he would not look out of place at all in the best Brazilian teams, which is one of the highest compliments. I would rate him along with Liam, too, among the best players to come out of Ireland. If I had to pick the three best players in the history of the Republic, two of them would be McGrath and Brady.

Then there was Denis Irwin, who could also have played in any team in the world. Again when you think of players of Denis' quality, you realise that at various times, Jack had a squad that was capable not just of qualifying for major tournaments but of going all the way and winning one of them. It was particularly unfortunate that they didn't qualify for the 1992 European Championship, losing out in the qualifying group by a point to England, at a time when several of the Republic's players were individually better than their England counterparts – certainly Packie Bonner, Denis Irwin, Paul McGrath, Ray Houghton and Roy Keane would have been in any well-run England team of that time. The Republic team that drew 3–3 in Poland in that group, after being 3–1 ahead, included Denis Irwin, Steve Staunton, David O'Leary, Paul McGrath, Kevin Moran, Ray Houghton,

Andy Townsend, Kevin Sheedy and Roy Keane. Who knows how far they would have gone in that tournament, which was famously won by Denmark.

Denis was always understated in his play, and I say that as a compliment. He would look like he was strolling through a game, but he was very quick. So when he was on the ball, he looked very relaxed, which might have given the impression that he could be caught in possession. But then he would release the ball, again with no fuss. Like most top-class players, when a burst of speed was called for, he had it. It was because of that quickness that he was able to have that apparently casual manner. You see other players who always look like they're sprinting; Denis, by contrast, always looked in control.

You wouldn't see Denis doing anything to attract attention to himself on the pitch, for the wrong reasons. He was not a 'character'. He was just a brilliant player. You won't see Denis on *Strictly Come Dancing*, but unlike the sort of 'characters' who find their way onto those programmes, Denis was a real player.

He could play on the right or the left side, a real team player, an intelligent lad. You need a certain mentality, a certain temperament, to be able to play in that position, and not to be getting the glory while your team-mates like Cantona and Beckham are becoming superstars. Denis' contribution to Manchester United was just as important as any of them, but in that unfussy way of his he got on with the job, doing it well, doing it professionally. Getting the ball and giving it, nice and simple, nice and quick. He was a lovely distributor of the ball, and a good dead-ball kicker – Denis could score a penalty, keeping his cool when all around him were losing theirs.

Ronnie Whelan was another player whose brilliance was perhaps not fully acknowledged because he played in such a dominant team. At Liverpool, he was one of those unsung heroes like Steve Nicol who were not praised as much as Dalglish, Souness or Hansen, probably because there's only a certain amount that can be written about any one team, and the media is happy enough with the big names. So in an odd way, if Ronnie had played for, say, Coventry City, he might have been a bigger name in England than he was. And if he had been English, he would surely have played for the national team, which would further have raised his profile. But I don't think Ronnie cared about that.

Whatever about his credentials as a possible England player, under Jack he was never even sure of his place in the Irish team, and he played only a few minutes as a substitute at Italia '90. Though he got some very valuable goals for us, he didn't get as many caps as he should have done. At Liverpool, there were no doubts about him. He was a good pro, he got goals for Liverpool too, defended well for them, played in an intelligent way. When he went to Liverpool, he had learned the culture of the club, the level of professionalism that was required, the attitude to winning things. In any job, in any walk of life, there is a culture that you absorb and, at Liverpool at that time, it was all very purposeful, there was a work ethic even in training. If Ronnie had gone to a club that did not have that culture – maybe Spurs – he might have been adversely affected by that. Many players would have been, but in the case of Ronnie I think he already had a professional approach before he went to Liverpool. And he just became one of them. I played with his father, Ronnie Whelan Senior, who was himself a very good player. So Ronnie was born into the game.

Some say that if Paul Gascoigne had gone to a club like Liverpool instead of Spurs, the club's culture might have been the making of him. But somehow with Gazza, I don't think so. And there is always a chance that a player who comes into a successful culture can exert such a strong influence in the wrong way, he can start to weaken it. For Ronnie, it was second nature to get on with the job, to get it done for the benefit of the team, to approach everything in the right way, with dedication. As one of the former Liverpool greats of that era put it to me, 'There was no fucking nonsense at Liverpool.'

I am also aware of how highly Ronnie was rated by the more celebrated Liverpool players. He was particularly noted for being in good defensive positions if they had the ball, for reading it well. He could cover the ground, he could break up attacks, and he could get you a goal. He was a good header, an all-round player.

At Everton, Kevin Sheedy was part of the team that did so well in the mid-1980s, winning the league twice, the FA Cup and the Cup Winners' Cup. He proved to be a good player for us too, a naturally left-sided player – there are not many of them around. During that period of success – the last time they have enjoyed such a spell – Everton could depend on

Sheedy to give them that width. He wouldn't go past players, but he was a very valuable player for them on the left side of midfield. They could depend on him there.

He could make goals and score goals, he was an excellent crosser. Kevin didn't lose the ball, he had a very good shot in his left foot, and he had a good attitude. Howard Kendall had put together a strong side there, with Peter Reid, Andy Gray, Graeme Sharp, Trevor Steven, Dave Watson and goalkeeper Neville Southall, who was outstanding for years. Sheedy was part of all that, he was used to winning ways, to that work ethic, and he brought that to Ireland. He also brought one of the great moments of Italia '90, the famous equaliser against England in Cagliari.

If Kevin Sheedy was a natural on the left, Ray Houghton was equally natural on the right side. Like Sheedy, he was not a winger, as such, more of an all-rounder, a midfield player who would get wide for you. Ray had a good football brain, he worked hard, won the ball well, he was bright. I actually tried to sign him when I was manager at West Bromwich Albion and Ray was a young player at Fulham. He had been recommended to me, and he came up to West Brom so that I could show him around the place. He ended up signing for Oxford United with whom he went on to win the League Cup, scoring the second goal at Wembley in a 3–0 defeat of QPR. And then he went to Liverpool and fitted immediately into the Liverpool way. Generally if you get a good lad, a good player who goes into that sort of environment, it makes him a better player. And this is what happened with Ray, who also proved to be terrific for Ireland.

While Ronnie Whelan had played mostly on the right for the Republic before the arrival of Ray, Ronnie could play in the middle as well. Some lads play on the right side but prefer to play somewhere else. Ray had found his niche there. He was fit, he covered the ground and he could keep going. He had the good technique of a natural footballer. Ray had tremendous energy and that brightness which meant you didn't have to tell him things twice.

Andy Townsend was not as comfortable on the ball as Ray. I never saw him as a natural midfield player, but one who got forward from midfield. He was another lad with a good attitude, who covered the ground well, had a good shot in his left foot, worked hard. As an attacking midfield player, he would also get you a few goals. Sometimes he would get ahead of the ball but that was OK, you needed a balance. Around his own box or in midfield Andy wouldn't fiddle around, as Jack would say. Jack wouldn't want you to fiddle around there, because he was scared you might lose it.

Andy was a good servant for the Republic, and so too was Gary Kelly. At Leeds United, Gary was one of only ten players who have played more than 500 games. He was one of the quickest lads I've ever seen, a full-back with that really natural pace that meant he could go on the overlap, get away from defenders and get a cross in – he had actually started off as a forward. And if someone got behind him, he was quick enough to be able to recover. But he was not just fast, he was well balanced, a very good player. His nephew, Ian Harte, was not nearly as fast, but Ian has also had an extraordinary career, which looked like it was coming to a close at Carlisle United until he got a second wind with Reading, which eventually took him back to the Premier League. He is also an excellent dead-ball kicker.

John Aldridge was so extraordinary, there was probably no one quite like him, not just for the Republic but in all my time in the game. For the Republic, he was asked to play in a way that didn't suit him, running into the corners after balls that had been played over the top. So the Republic was the only side in which Aldridge played that he didn't score as many goals as he might have done, or didn't get to display his unique skills. And when I say unique, I really mean it here. John Aldridge was one of the most unusual players I have ever seen. He was a little bit awkward around the ball, not a classy player in that sense and, like other clinical finishers, such as Ian Rush, he didn't contribute a great deal outside the box – Rush indeed contributed a fair bit more than Aldridge, in general play. But inside the box Aldrdge was unbelievable, providing the ultimate proof that finishing is an art form in itself, quite separate from the rest of the game.

It's a bit like an ordinary golfer who is a great putter. In general, putting has nothing to do with the game of golf in general, and some people just have a genius for it that is unrelated to their overall ability at the sport. John Aldridge was a bit like that. A player like Kenny Dalglish was great all round. You'd expect him to be able to finish because of his perfect technique in all areas of the game. Jimmy Greaves, such a master in front of goal, could beat players outside the box too, had beautiful control, could do it on his own, going past three, four or five players to score. By contrast, you could watch Aldridge outside the box and you'd think that he couldn't play at all. Next thing you know he is inside the box, making room for himself, chipping the keeper, sliding it into the net – a world-class striker.

With Aldridge, I think there was a bigger difference between what he could do outside the box and what he could do inside the box than any other player I have seen. I recall being at a function at Tranmere Rovers, where Aldridge played towards the end of his career, and being made aware of the amazing number of goals he had scored during his time in the game. He scored seventy goals in 170 appearances for Newport County, seventy-two goals in 114 appearances for Oxford United, fifty in eighty-three for Liverpool, thirty-three in sixty-three for Real Sociedad, and 138 in 243 for Tranmere Rovers. With nineteen for the Republic along the way. A remarkable player.

Tony Cascarino was a big, honest, robust centre-forward and in many parts of his career he was the total opposite to Aldridge. He was not a natural finisher, he did not have that strange gift and, at times, he could be quite poor inside the box. But he worked endlessly outside the box, contributing in that way. I never saw John Aldridge losing his confidence in the way that some strikers do, up to and including Fernando Torres. Whereas Cascarino was very streaky in that regard. I always felt he couldn't quite believe that he was playing at such a high level, and at those times when his confidence was low, he could look awkward. But I liked Cascarino, he was a goer, always willing. And he was always brave, going for headers. He was not prolific, but he got a few important goals for us.

Jason McAteer got one of the most important goals of them all, the winner against the Netherlands at Lansdowne Road which put us through to the 2002 World Cup. Jason was a useful player for us, who could play in a few positions, always lively, with a good attitude.

Niall Quinn was never found wanting either in that regard. Niall was very intelligent, with a good knowledge of the game. His instincts were those of a natural footballer, with his sense of when to lay the ball off, what weight to put on a pass, when to release it. And his positional sense can best be illustrated by comparing it with that of, say, Emile Heskey, who, when he headed the ball, would often just head it to no one in particular. Niall, and players like him, would be having a little look while the ball was in the air, in order to direct it more accurately. The goal he laid on for Robbie Keane against Germany in the World Cup in Japan was a perfect example of this, and at Sunderland he formed a partnership with Kevin Phillips in which he did that sort of thing all the time.

A big fellow who was not that well co-ordinated, Niall couldn't always do what he wanted to do, even though he knew the possibilities. He could see it, but he couldn't always execute it. So on certain days he could look like the best in the world, and on others he could look like the worst. But he was a very valuable player. When he first came on the scene at Arsenal, Niall was a lanky sort of a lad. But he got stronger as his career developed at Manchester City, becoming an effective target man. He was always a trier, having a go, but now he was able to hold centre-halves off, out-muscle them when he had to. And with that intelligence of his, he knew when to go to the near post, when to go to the far post, always trying to do the right things. Niall was a big player for Ireland.

Robbie Keane, who took over from Niall as our leading scorer, is another of those players who would clearly come under the category of goal scorer, the specialist skill that gave him fifty-three goals for Ireland by the end of Euro 2012. That was his main contribution to any of the teams he played with, a major contribution. He didn't make many goals for other people but he was always a threat inside the box, with his coolnesss and confidence. I recall in particular a match in Cyprus, when he was having a nightmare – and then he scored the winner for the Republic. No matter what he was doing in general play, if you were putting money on someone to score a goal, you'd have to back Robbie.

I think if he had gone to Liverpool as a young fellow, rather than Wolves, he might have learned his overall trade a bit better. Instead, he kept moving to different clubs in the earlier part of his career, which only made it harder to learn his trade. But he is very talented, with good technique and an exuberance in his play, along with a good football brain. And, anyway, you very seldom get the complete player. That goal-scoring record stands up, and for the Republic some of them were very important goals. Apart from the sort of goal he could score against Cyprus out of nothing, I think of those late equalisers in the World Cup in Japan against Germany and Spain, the latter a penalty that Robbie stuck away under the most extreme pressure after Iker Casillas had saved an earlier penalty from Ian Harte. In those moments, he showed that he was a top player. And if you were putting together an all-time Irish team, you would have to consider him strongly.

The responsibility for scoring goals for the Republic will shift to Kevin Doyle and Shane Long. The fact that they are from Wexford and Tipperary respectively is itself a good thing, a sign of how far the game has come in this country. In my time, and certainly before Italia '90, you would never hear of players coming from those parts. Yet we now have players of the quality of Long and Doyle from these more 'rural' areas, and in general we are producing promising young players in greater numbers than they are in Scotland, Wales or Northern Ireland. There is probably more association football played in Kerry today than Gaelic football – an amazing transformation. Shane Long used to play hurling, which wouldn't do him any harm in terms of the physical side of the game. He is strong in the air, skilful and he protects the ball well. Kevin Doyle has been a bit unlucky with injuries, and in the fact that since he has joined Wolves they have been struggling all the time. He has been up there as a lone striker, which is a very difficult role even in a successful team. If he was in a team that was creating more chances, we would see that he is not just a good-hearted lad, but a very good player.

Damien Duff, too, has been a really good lad. I have never seen him do anything but his best for club or country. And on certain days, he has looked really brilliant, with his dribbling skills, his ability to take players on and beat them, before sending in a dangerous cross. But because he lacks positional sense, he doesn't get into those situations often enough. When he receives the ball, he is usually facing his own goal, which means that he has do all sorts of tricks to get himself out of trouble. That is the mental image that many of us have of Damien, rather than him being one-on-one with the full-back, doing the sort of damge that we know he can do.

The thing that has always baffled me is that it would not have been too difficult to teach him that positional sense – essentially it's about knowing how to receive the ball, which for a winger involves staying as wide as you can and not getting in front of the ball if it's on the other side of the pitch, whether your team is in possession or not. It's the sort of thing that isn't really that hard to put right. Yet not even Mourinho at Chelsea did it with Damien, though it must be said that Mourinho has a funny way of using wingers. It isn't the orthodox way, he wants them in a bit from the touchline. So Damien had that very good season at Chelsea when they won the Premiership, without really improving his positional sense as a winger. Not that I want to be too hard on him. I think Damien is a really good kid and I have a lot of respect for him. He deserves his 100 caps, his success in the Premier League and everything that goes with it.

John O'Shea has been a good all-round player who has had an unusual career. He was prepared to be an understudy at Manchester United, though he was unlucky with injuries too when he became more established in the side. The fact that he never made a fuss was ideal for Alex Ferguson, but not necessarily for John O'Shea. I feel that for the sake of his career, he should have moved from United earlier. There is nothing better than playing week in and week out to make the most of your ability. And O'Shea had plenty of that, at full-back or at centre-back – he could also put on a show in midfield.

Richard Dunne has been another terrific player for the Irish team, another very talented lad. I think he lost his way a couple of times early in his career at Everton and Manchester City and then he buckled down as all young lads can do. He became an outstanding player with all the qualities of a top centre-half. He was exceptionally quick, with good feet for a big lad, and he was good in the air. Richard had great heart and determination and he would throw his body on the line. He was a hero for the Irish team even before his amazing performance in Moscow in which he and Shay Given kept doing remarkable things to keep the Russians out. Playing for his club week to week, I'm not sure if he concentrates all the time, as much as he concentrates a lot of the time. As a player, you have a certain expectation of yourself, and for Ireland I think he has fulfilled that. I think he has found it more difficult to sustain it all the time at club level, but his contribution to the Republic has been beyond question.

From a great football family, Richard is probably unfortunate that when it comes to putting together an all-time Irish team, his position of centre-half is so strongly represented. But at his best, he could have played with the likes of McGrath in that team. He is up there with them.

Shay Given was on his own, our best ever keeper. He has been one of the top keepers in England over a number of years and, until the arrival of Joe Hart, would undoubtedly have been the undisputed first choice for the England team – when you consider that David James held that position for some time, you see the strength of the case for Given here. Luckily enough, Ireland had him instead, and it is questionable whether we would have qualifed for the 2002 World Cup or the 2012 European Championship without his world-class abilities.

He was probably a bit more agile than Packie Bonner, and certainly a better kicker. And like Packie, and Alan Kelly before him, along with his class, he had a tremendous attitude all the way through. People wonder why Arsène Wenger never signed Shay for Arsenal when they desperately needed a reliable keeper, and I can only say that I don't know why either. He had the consistency that they needed, a calmness. He made big saves and he got on with the job. And at Newcastle he had a lot more to do than a keeper such as Edwin van der Sar would have to do at Manchester United. Of course, van der Sar had to be good to begin with, but because he was less likely to concede a goal with a team of United's quality, after that he only had to be competent. And so the reputation of a van der Sar grows in the Premier League. In Ireland, in terms of what he did for the national team over the years, the reputation of Shay Given is secure.

Which brings us to Roy Keane. I have often heard certain players being described as sunshine boys. They're the sort of lads who, when you're 3–0 up, are saying, 'Give me the ball.' When the contest is over, that's when they do their stuff. At that point, in fact, not only do they want the ball, as we say in the game, 'they want to eat the fucking ball'.

Roy was the opposite of a sunshine boy. Always in a game of football there is a contest. Sometimes you can be two or three goals up after fiften minutes and, if you are any good at all, it is effectively over. But a game can go through very different phases. You can be 2–0 up, it gets back to 2–2, and you have to fight again. You were dominating, then they got back into it with a corner kick or something. Now you are at the height of the battle, a point that comes in every game. This is when the real players show themselves. They show their character, their attitude of no surrender. This is when they get on the ball. Keane was at his best in those situations. And, oddly enough, if you were leading 3–0 and coasting, Keane wasn't really much good to you. It just didn't get him going. He would leave that to the sunshine boys.

For those boys, perhaps the worst scenario of all is when you're playing at home against a team that you're expected to beat. You're 1–0 down and the crowd is getting impatient, to say the least. That's when the sunshine boys don't want to get on the ball, because they know that if they make a mistake, the crowd will be on to them. But the real players will get on the ball regardless of the crowd's reaction. In fact, they will go against the crowd if they have to. Again, in those circumstances, Keane was at his sharpest.

This is what made him great, his attitude at the height of battle, or when a team needed someone to drag them back into a game. Especially an important game. Of all the players I have seen and the players that I knew, Keane is the man I would go to in that situation. He was the one who did it most often, and who did it better than anyone else.

When Keane arrived from Nottingham Forest, Paul Ince was the all-action player at Manchester United. But Keane was better at doing what Ince did than Ince himself. And he didn't fancy himself as much as Ince did – he did not want to be called the 'Guvnor', and all that rubbish. Steve Bruce and Gary Pallister in defence got on with the job without needing any nicknames, and as for Keane himself, everything was for the team. When United were 3–0 up, he wouldn't exactly be redundant, but he would be at his least effective. That was Keane's personality. I don't know Roy Keane except what I saw on the pitch, so I am talking about his personality as a player. The satisfaction for him seemed to come from that natural drive of his, and the way he could drive other people. It didn't come from playing the ball around when the match was won. Nor was Keane a player like Bobby Charlton, who could get on the ball and distribute it in a classy way. Keane's control was good, his distribution was all right, but not adventurous. I can think of other midfield players who had more to their game in that sense. Yet they did not have that drive of his, that quality which made him invaluable to any team he played in.

I think of the 1996 FA Cup final in which United beat Liverpool 1–0 with a late goal by Eric Cantona, to win the Double. Naturally Cantona got all the headlines, and was made Man of the Match. And yet if it hadn't been for Keane, and the way that he played, I'd say that United would have been three goals down by then. It was a tough, hard game, and he was outstanding in the way that he kept them going, kept them in the game – which gave Cantona the chance to score what was a spectacular winner.

There was only one Man of the Match for me. And Keane did that many times for United, and for Ireland, making himself into a great player. He had a good first touch, but more than that, he was exceptionally quick. When Manchester United were at their most vulnerable, when the other team had the ball, he would cover the ground brilliantly. He had to be quick to do that. He didn't do any of it because of his affection for his team-mates, and for all we know they may have been frightened of him. But whatever drove him to play the way he did, it doesn't matter. All that matters is that he did it, and that he was hugely effective in doing it.

On the field, it made no difference if he was popular with his team-mates or unpopular. The important thing was that, when everyone else was drooping, he became stronger. There is no doubt he would have the respect of the other players – the highest respect. As for their affection, who knows? Some of the best players in the world have been the biggest pricks in the world. Which does not really matter to the other players or to the supporters in terms of valuing their contribution on the pitch. Then again, some of the great players such as Pelé and Maradona and Messi have had the affection of their fellow players. So you can be a leader and still be popular.

It's not essential to have that affection of your colleagues but, if you do have it, it can make it even better. I'm not sure if Keane had that. And I feel that he may regret missing out on that World Cup in 2002, just as Ireland missed him in Japan. I would still say that Keane, Liam Brady and Paul McGrath are the top three Irish players I have seen. Again, they are all different, united by that common thread of greatness.

I was very lucky in my career to play with the likes of Billy Bremner and Norman Hunter and the Leeds lads in general who, at the height of the battle, were never found wanting. I played with Nobby Stiles too, and he would be up there in that regard. But if I was in a battle to win a match, to save my life, and I had to choose one player to be by my side, I think that I would want to have Roy Keane there. That is the highest compliment I can pay him.

15

Bobby Charlton — the Greatest

In April 2011, there was a major BBC documentary on Sir Bobby Charlton, in which it was generally agreed by all the distinguished football men who contributed to it that Bobby was perhaps the greatest player of them all.

Personally I don't think you can compare the great players of one era with the great players of another era in that way, so I have always put it like this – having played with Bobby during my early years at Manchester United, and against him many times after I left Old Trafford, I can say that Bobby was the greatest player I ever played with or against. So I was happy to see his career being celebrated by that BBC programme.

But there was still something strange about it, at least in the timing of it. Apparently it took the best part of forty years for everyone to fully realise that Bobby, who retired as a player in the mid-1970s, really was up there with Pelé and Cruyff and Maradona and George Best. There has been no shortage of TV documentaries about those players – in fact there has been a whole industry dedicated to George – but it took a bit longer for the full truth about Bobby to dawn.

Around the time of that documentary, there was also a film made for the BBC about the Munich disaster, in which Bobby was one of the main characters – the other was the assistant manager Jimmy Murphy, who had missed the trip to Munich. And while it was good to see Murphy finally getting his due as well, I found it odd that the actor playing him, David Tennant, who is also Dr Who, bore no resemblance at all to the actual Murphy – an odd state of affairs, since the actual Murphy looked so distinctive, almost like a movie actor himself, maybe one of James Cagney's henchmen in an old gangster film.

I was also put off by scenes of United's centre-half Mark Jones smoking a pipe, something I never recalled any of the United players doing back then, and a particularly dreadful invention as Jones appeared to be smoking his pipe in the tunnel while the two teams were ready to go out onto the pitch. The makers of the film seemed unaware that this might be disrespectful to the players of that time, that Mark Jones and Duncan Edwards and all the rest of them were really good pros who might not welcome these misrepresentations. There was a scene of Bobby unable to sleep on the night before his debut, arriving down to Old Trafford at about 3 o'clock in the morning, another strange piece of fiction which made me question the movie as a whole. But despite all that, it was still encouraging to see Bobby as the hero, getting most of the attention for a change.

Maybe the lack of proper recognition over the years is partly because Bobby comes across as a fairly normal person in comparison to some of the other giants of the game. Maybe he was too 'straight' in his personality to attract the sort of attention that other great players have received, to their advantage in terms of fame but perhaps to their detriment as people. He didn't always get the publicity of a Maradona or a George Best because his personal life did not have that element of tragedy which would raise his profile for the wrong reasons.

Indeed, George Best was effectively out of the game at an age when his prodigious abilities should have been taking him to new heights. He had become a superstar very quickly, and to some extent his stardom reflected badly on Bobby. In the spirit of the time, to the outside world George represented the present and future, while Bobby seemed to belong vaguely to the past. Bobby was just a great player who didn't cause any trouble. With his modest demeanour, he seemed to have more in common with Stanley Matthews and Tom Finney than with those who came after them. Bobby didn't look like a pop star – in fact, he was already going bald in his mid-twenties. And this made him look like the sort of person who would disapprove strongly of almost everything that George was doing to enjoy himself.

In football that special trio of Best, Charlton and Law may be joined together in immortality, but back in the 1960s it was Best with his charisma who was the idol of the press and the general public, followed closely by Law, who was not only a great player, he looked like a modern young man – or at least he looked a lot more modern than Bobby did. Yet even at the time, within the game, many football men including myself held the view that Bobby was in truth the greatest they had known. And it is a view that has only become stronger with the passing of time.

Of course this is just my perspective, and we must always remember that. Sir Alex Ferguson was on that BBC programme too, and he couldn't speak highly enough of Bobby Charlton. He genuinely believes that Bobby was a magnificent player. Yet the same Alex Ferguson said that Cristiano Ronaldo was the best player in the world, at a time when, in my opinion at least, he wasn't even the best player at Manchester United – that was Paul Scholes. As for Ronaldo himself, who certainly regards himself as a great player, in an ideal world anyone who puts his own name forward for such an accolade should be automatically excluded from consideration.

Bobby Charlton never made such claims for himself. And maybe if he had, he'd be more of a first choice when the all-time greats are being discussed. Because he has never been involved in controversy, perhaps he's been somewhat taken for granted. Perhaps that apparent normality has fooled some people into thinking that the things he could do on the pitch were pretty normal too. But right from the start, Bobby was a player of the most abnormal ability.

I saw Bobby for the first time when I went to Manchester United at the age of fourteen. He was seventeen, and I could see that he was special. It didn't take that long for him to reach the first eleven, and in fact he was established in the first team just before the Munich disaster. I can also say for certain that Dennis Viollet, like Bobby a survivor of Munich, was one of the best players I ever played with.

Again you don't hear a lot about Dennis. Perhaps it's because the Busby Babes who died at Munich assumed such a legendary status, and rightly so, that Dennis' name is not spoken with the same sense of awe. Before Munich, he was a goal-scoring inside-forward with an excellent positional sense – afterwards he played as a targetman. Even during his career, he didn't get the credit he should have, playing only twice for England – he was at his best at the time of the Selection Committee, who didn't know how good he was, and when he was eventually picked, it was about three years too late. But it was a joy to play alongside him.

His career ended a bit prematurely, perhaps because he didn't look after himself properly. Dennis would have been described at the time as a bit of a 'playboy'. And ultimately he ended up at Stoke City, which tells us that the more glamorous the life of the player off the park, the less glamorous his football life tends to become. But he was brilliant for United, especially after Munich. As was the young lad who had just broken into the first team at the time, Bobby Charlton.

In fact, Bobby was more than brilliant in that terrible time just after Munich. His contribution on the field was so immense that he probably did more than any other individual to keep the spirit of Manchester United alive – though a lot of credit must also go to Jimmy Murphy, not just for taking over the running of the club while Matt Busby was recovering from his injuries, but for being a huge influence on Bobby from the time that Bobby joined the club. Certainly Bobby himself always maintained that he owed a great deal to Murphy, who had such a deep knowledge of the game. So it seems a strange thing to say that Bobby's own knowledge of the game wasn't great. But that is how it seemed to me.

His knowledge of the game wasn't great – but it didn't seem to matter. I played with Bobby for a few seasons, and I don't remember ever having a conversation with him to analyse a game, one in which we'd look back and we'd say, 'You could have done this, or you should have done that.' He didn't analyse what he did, and maybe he didn't know how he did it – something that would have bothered me a lot more during my playing career than it does now.

As a player, trying to learn my trade, I felt that even for the most talented individuals, a deep knowledge of the game and how it worked was the big thing. Yet from my own experience I could see that Bobby defied that theory, and that it didn't detract in any way from his obvious brilliance.

So I always felt that Bobby Charlton was a man of instinct rather than analysis. Bobby didn't have a nasty streak, and indeed there'd be some in the game who might wish he did, but then his overall attitude and ability was so exceptional that it made him a great player anyway. I never saw Bobby when he wasn't trying, or wasn't looking for the ball if he was having a bad game. In some games, he might not have been having the best of times, but still you would never question his moral courage. He was very quick, and a great dribbler, but what separated him was his shooting skills. Bobby could threaten the goal from thirty-five or forty yards out, with either foot. He could win a match with one outrageous shot. He could do it on his own.

But he didn't talk about it. When I played with Billy Bremner at Leeds, we would be chatting a lot, both on and off the pitch. Always there would be things happening that we felt we needed to discuss. For example, Billy was inclined to get forward a bit early, especially if we were losing. So we'd talk about that. If you raised anything of that nature with Bobby, or just made a remark about his position on the pitch at a particular moment, he had very little interest in it, and eventually he'd probably just tell you to get lost. He did it his own way. And, of course, it was so often a very good way, which worked for him and for the team.

Bobby wasn't a sunshine boy. But there would be an element within the game that we might call the kill-your-granny-to-win brigade, and Bobby wouldn't come into that category. These completely ruthless lads would say that 'he couldn't tackle a hot dinner' because he didn't have a nasty streak, and they wouldn't be wrong about that. They would have great respect for him in many ways, but this would be a criticism. Maybe to be more accurate you could call it a reserved criticism.

It tends to arise when people are picking their best eleven, and they say, 'Look, the best way to judge that is you've got to go to some place like Argentina, where you know it's going to be tough, or maybe behind the old Iron Curtain. And you're playing for your life. Who are you going to pick?'

Certain names would be mentioned straight away for such an assignment – there would be Norman Hunter, Dave Mackay, Cliff Jones, Bobby Collins, and I would add John Robertson, though John wasn't exactly a killer either. And you might go for Denis Law rather than Jimmy Greaves, because Denis may be remembered almost entirely for his goal-scoring brilliance but he was also a very aggressive player, and in fact in some circumstances he would take your head off.

Yes, for such a trip to the wilds of Argentina, you would need these hard nuts, the gladiatorial types. And there's nothing wrong with that because, after all, in any match there's a battle out there that you're going to have to win. Writers will condemn players with that 'nasty streak', but I know as a player, for and against, that football is not played by philosophers, it is played by warriors. Footballers are not worldly people – if they were, they wouldn't be able to play with the passion that is needed. You can't be too worldly, because then you'd be too intelligent for the game to matter that much. Some writers want it all. They want players to be men of the world and to be warriors. But when it really matters, you'll want Roy Keane on your side, because he wouldn't be the most complete or the most well-rounded person in the world, and neither would Bryan Robson, and neither would John Terry or Billy Bremner or Dave Mackay, but you'd still want them down there in Argentina if your life depended on it.

Which brings us to this very hard question – for such an assignment, would you pick Graeme Souness rather than Bobby Charlton? While the kill-your-granny-to-win brigade would hesitate before making their selection, eventually they would probably go for Souness because of that reserved criticism of theirs about Bobby – basically, he couldn't 'do' anybody.

And physical intimidation is a part of the game. It stops your opponents being relaxed when the ball comes to them. In the modern era, it is said that Manchester United wouldn't have been great without a Roy Keane or a Bryan Robson, and that they miss that sort of player today – but then who wouldn't miss them? When I was at United, at the age of eighteen, nineteen or twenty, I didn't want to be thinking about the more ruthless aspects of the game, the stuff they'd be doing down there in Argentina. In fact, I think Matt Busby felt that there wasn't enough 'devil' in me. But then he had other players who were not lacking in that regard. Matt may have been a gentleman and a charmer, but he had Nobby Stiles, Paddy Crerand, Bill Foulkes and the aforementioned Denis Law out there, and they had any amount of 'devil' in them. Because Matt knew it was very hard to succeed without that.

I had a lot more 'devil' in me when I was playing with Leeds. But even in the early days, while I wasn't as aggressive as others, I wouldn't be frightened out of a game either. And the same could be said for Bobby. He wasn't able to be a digger, but if someone had a go at him, I never saw him shirk. There were some players who would be tackled hard early on, and that would be the end of them. 'Let this lad know you're playing,' we would be told, and it usually worked. So I think that Bobby was aware of the benefit of having a nasty streak, without actually being able to do it. He had a great fascination, for example, with Jimmy Scoular, who, apart from all his other qualities, was a very hard nut indeed. Bobby saw him playing as a young boy, and saw others who had equally tough reputations, and he admired them. But it just wasn't in him to copy the darker side of their game.

Not that that stopped him becoming a great player. Which he did. Of that there is no doubt. Playing with Bobby, I could see that he was so gifted, he could do it on his own. We were told to let it go simply, let it go quick. There were times when I would be in a great position to receive it, and just when I'd be saying, 'For fuck's sake, Bob', because Bobby hadn't delivered it, he would be past three players and would be threatening the goal. If he was at Barcelona today, he could do what Xavi and Iniesta between them can do – Bobby could go past players, so you didn't need that intricate passing. At Leeds, Billy Bremner and I needed each other, but Bobby just needed good helpers like Nobby Stiles and Paddy Crerand at United, or Alan Ball with England. The rest he could do by himself.

Looking back, the fact that Bobby achieved all he did in the game is even more admirable when you consider that he won the World Cup and the European Cup and the league and the FA Cup without 'doing' anyone. And that this implied no weakness on his part, that his moral courage was still beyond question.

For all these things, in my experience as a player, Bobby Charlton was not just great – he was the greatest.

John Giles' Dream Teams

Best
Republic of Ireland
Team

Shay Given

Denis Irwin

Charlie Hurley

Paul McGrath

Tony Dunne

Ray Houghton

Ronnie Whelan

Roy Keane

Liam Brady

Frank Stapleton

Don Givens

My Dream Matches

Teams I would love to see playing each other.

World XI		World XI
Iker Casillas	v	Peter Schmeichel
(*Spain*)		(*Denmark*)
Carlos Alberto	v	Lilian Thuram
(*Brazil*)		(*France*)
Franz Beckenbauer	v	Giacinto Facchetti
(*West Germany*)		(*Italy*)
Franco Baresi	v	Fabio Cannavaro
(*Italy*)		(*Italy*)
Paolo Maldini	v	Marcel Desailly
(*Italy*)		(*France*)
Jairzinho	v	Luis Figo
(*Brazil*)		(*Portugal*)
Xavi Hernandez	v	Andrea Pirlo
(*Spain*)		(*Italy*)
Günter Netzer	v	Zinedine Zidane
(*West Germany*)		(*France*)
Andrés Iniesta	v	Johan Cruyff
(*Spain*)		(*The Netherlands*)
Lionel Messi	v	Diego Maradona
(*Argentina*)		(*Argentina*)
Pelé	v	Ferenc Puskas
(*Brazil*)		(*Hungary*)

Great Britain & Ireland XI   Great Britain & Ireland XI

Pat Jennings	v	Gordon Banks
(Northern Ireland)		*(England)*
Denis Irwin	v	Paul Madeley
(Republic of Ireland)		*(England)*
John Charles	v	Paul McGrath
(Wales)		*(Republic of Ireland)*
Bobby Moore	v	Alan Hansen
(England)		*(Scotland)*
Stuart Pearce	v	Terry Cooper
(England)		*(England)*
George Best	v	Billy Bremner
(Northern Ireland)		*(Scotland)*
Bobby Charlton	v	Graeme Souness
(England)		*(Scotland)*
Dave Mackay	v	Paul Scholes
(Scotland)		*(England)*
John Robertson	v	Liam Brady
(Scotland)		*(Republic of Ireland)*
Denis Law	v	Kevin Keegan
(Scotland)		*(England)*
Jimmy Greaves	v	Kenny Dalglish
(England)		*(Scotland)*

Substitutes   Substitutes

Roy Keane	v	Mike Summerbee
(Republic of Ireland)		*(England)*
Bryan Robson	v	Francis Lee
(England)		*(England)*
Jimmy Johnstone	v	Peter Lorimer
(Scotland)		*(Scotland)*
Norman Hunter	v	Eddie Gray
(England)		*(Scotland)*
Cliff Jones	v	Alan Ball
(Wales)		*(England)*
Ian Rush	v	Johnny Haynes
(Wales)		*(England)*

Permission Acknowledgements

Photographs © Getty Images except © Colorsport (Section 1, p.7, bottom photo; section 3, p.3; section 3, p.4, top photo; section 3, p.6, bottom right photo; section 3, p.8, top photo)

Every effort has been made to fulfil requirements with regard to reproducing copyright material. The author and publisher will be glad to rectify any omissions at the earliest opportunity.

Index

Players, managers, teams, competitions and organisations

Declan Lynch began his writing career at the age of seventeen with Ireland's rock and roll magazine *Hot Press* and now writes for the *Sunday Independent*. He is the author of several works of fiction and non-fiction, including the acclaimed novel *The Rooms*. He also worked with John Giles on his bestselling autobiography *A Football Man*.